How to Live Well

-

Chic Inspiration

-

How to be Slim and Healthy

FIONA FERRIS

Copyright © 2015 Fiona Ferris
All rights reserved.

ISBN-13: 978-1515333272
ISBN-10: 1515333272

DEDICATION

This book is dedicated to the lovely readers of my blog How to be Chic. Thank you for joining me in the pursuit of a simple and beautiful way of life.

Contents

Introduction 9

Chapter 1. Looking forward to future plans 11

    On making the most of time 11

    Embracing a new year 15

    Dreaming up the ideal life 17

Chapter 2. 21

Nurturing yourself 21

    Boudoir time 21

    Quiet time 22

    Low-stress secrets 23

    How to feel better 27

    Recipe for a good night's sleep 30

Chapter 3. 32

Living a life of style 32

    Living a chic life 32

    Elegance is refusal 35

Chapter 4. 37

Chic habits *37*

    Go to bed earlier, get up earlier *37*

    How to stay young *39*

    Swapping stockpiling for tranquility *41*

    Cultivating calmness *42*

Chapter 5. .... *46*

Inspiration on living well *46*

    Living a small life *46*

    Living as our grandparents did *48*

    Kaizen *51*

    On living a low-key life *52*

    Simplicity manifesto *54*

    A life of luxury *55*

Chic Inspiration: *59*

Chapter 6. .... *61*

Favourite chic inspiration *61*

    Being feminine in everyday life *61*

    Being 'French' *64*

    Joie de vivre *67*

    Reasons to smile *68*

Ways to bring more French chic into your life 69

Living like a princess 72

A sensual life 75

Chapter 7. 79

Real life inspiration 79

An evening with Mireille 79

My trip to Paris 84

European men are different 86

True stories from Paris 87

Chapter 8. 89

Inspiration from books and magazines 89

True Pleasures 89

How to seduce 90

Supermarket Supermodel 94

How to be happy 95

The Paris Winter 98

Chapter 9. 101

Inspiration from movies and television 101

Downton Abbey 101

How to be a lady 103

A perfect afternoon on the sofa 106

Chapter 10 108

Reader Questions 108

   Reader Question #1 108

   Reader Question #2 111

Chapter 11 115

Inspiring words 115

   Desiderata 118

How to Be Slim and Healthy: 121

Chapter 12 123

Being slim 123

   Avoiding overeating 124

   Countdown to 40 126

   Becoming and staying slim 128

   More on slimming 131

   The secret to permanent slimness? 133

Chapter 13 137

The French approach to exercise 137

   Moving like a French woman 137

   Gaining more energy 140

How to make walking fun *141*

Chapter 14 .... *144*

Breakfast, Lunch and Dinner *144*

   My favourite chic breakfast *144*

   Chic lunches *146*

   La baguette *148*

   Best. Soup. Ever. *150*

   Comfort food for a Sunday evening *152*

   Enjoying cooking at home *155*

Chapter 15 .... *158*

On good health *158*

   A health schedule *158*

   How I became a non-drinker *161*

   Getting back into sorts *165*

A WORD FROM THE AUTHOR *169*

ABOUT THE AUTHOR *171*

How to Live Well:
Simple and practical inspiration to enjoy your everyday life

Introduction

The concept of living well is one of my favourite subjects to think about. It encompasses every part of our life – how we live in our home, how we go about our days, what we wear and what we eat. Who do we spend our time with and who do we choose to share the intimate parts of our life?

We don't just need to float along though, taking what comes to us in life like we have no choice in the matter. We can intentionally design our life to be exactly what we've already dreamed of in our mind. Yes, it takes more effort than going along with the status quo and what your neighbours, friends and family might be doing, but there is real value in asking yourself 'what do *I* want'. I used to think this was selfish, but now realise it's not serving anyone if you go along with someone else's plan.

You don't need to upend your current life though. You can start small and look at the way you do things and the kinds of activities you participate in. Do they add to your life or detract from it? What would you rather be doing, you know, in that far away hazy perfect dream life in the future that always seems *just* around the corner? I've got news for you, that mirage will always be out of our reach if we don't call it forward.

Yes, it can feel scary, knowing we have so much power, but I know from the wonderful ways in which I've stepped into the unknown so far, you gain results that are incredible. And by being creative there are many ways you can elevate your lifestyle without spending much at all.

Chapter 1.
Looking forward to future plans

Even though I endeavour to make living in the present my main focus, we need to plan for the future too. So why not make it fun and exciting to think about?

In addition, rather than only looking forward to the big things – a vacation overseas or a new house or car perhaps – it is also inspiring to consider all the little things that we do every day, and make those as enjoyable as possible too.

Let's dive in.

On making the most of time

My husband and I own and run a retail footwear business. At this stage we don't have any staff, and we are open seven days a week. I update our website and do the bookwork, my husband does the ordering. We both see sales representatives with samples and both work in the shop.

All of this means we don't get a ton of time off together, as the shop would have to be closed. We are happy with it this way for now and, believe it or not we do still have balance in our life. We very rarely take work home with us and we have days off during the week which I actually prefer. They aren't with each other, but we do spend time together at work (we enjoy each other's company and have fun together as well as complete our work tasks).

A day off during the week mostly means a day at home for me (my absolute favourite place to be) or if I have some errands (rare, as decluttering cures the urge to shop, especially with our tiny house) it's so good to go shopping when most other people are at work.

If on the rare occasion I have to go to a mall, there are often lots of retired couples walking around, along with mums and pre-schoolers. I often think how nice it would be to be retired. Having an orderly, stress-free life. Spending all day doing the things you want to do, preparing for a meal, going out and gathering ingredients, browsing the library shelves, tending things at home.

I know I'm too young to think about retirement by at least twenty years, but when I'm out walking I go past a big new retirement complex nearby (which is more 'apartments to buy' than a rest home) and on the street-side is a big bay window looking into their communal living room. It is decorated with sofas that look like the Something's Gotta Give movie house, in fact the whole property is very chic and stylish and new but looks classic.

There are retired people in there who, no matter when I walk past are always talking and laughing and socialising. It's not far from our shop and I have often wondered what the minimum age is to move in. My husband is keen too! I sometimes wonder if we don't have more in common with these people than friends our own age.

We have no children, we like a tipple before dinner, we don't hold rowdy parties, a soft jazz CD is the loudest thing we play, we like our own space, we watch English soap Coronation Street and we rarely eat out. Plus I knit. Gosh, maybe I really am an 85 year old on the inside. On reflection, I think we actually already live like we're retired (except that we go to work, a minor consideration).

I also really like the couples they use in retirement advertising. They are walking along a beach, the wife has jeans rolled up with a white shirt. She is slender and chic with a silver bob. Her husband is handsome and lean with salt and pepper hair (perhaps more pepper) and has jeans on also with a V-neck navy jersey. Very classic and I can definitely relate to their style!

Paris is a goal. We did not have a honeymoon when we married just over two years ago, and our next (first) overseas holiday will be our Paris honeymoon. I don't care when that is, it could be ten years away. If this trip includes NYC so much the better. But I also think about retirement as a goal. It's roughly twenty-five years away for me and my husband as here in New Zealand sixty-five is the retirement age.

I don't want to fritter away time and money on mindless living. I did that in my twenties and thirties. Now that I am approaching my forties I have realised we don't have endless years on this earth. I plan to enjoy my time and plan wisely for the future.

All of this may sound really selfish, me, me, me, my enjoyment. But I have served others in the past, by volunteering at the SPCA for about four years before we had our own business. I had to quit because I couldn't be in two places at once. I donate money to favourite causes. It used to be Automatic Payments from my bank account, now I donate as and when I want to.

I also am in the process of using up my wool odds and ends and practicing my crochet by making rugs for needy babies.

At my rate of crochet it could be a slow output but I'm doing something!

I also downloaded a knitting pattern from the SPCA for puppy sweaters. Apparently little abandoned puppies get extremely cold without their mother to warm them. So this is another plan for my wool scraps and tv time (I can't watch tv or a movie without knitting, crocheting, filing my nails etc. I get too fiddly and would likely go looking for something to eat).

So my goal for the next twenty-five years (and beyond) is to continue as I have started out:

Being healthy, strong and slender

Enjoying good, nutritious food cooked at home for the most part

Simplifying my life

Decluttering my home and paring down

Being a good steward of my money

Making the most of simple luxuries

Buying less but better quality, in food, clothing, furniture

Letting go of stressful notions that I can control the behaviour of others

Going with the flow

Nurturing my relationship with my husband – he comes before all other people in my life

Learn how to worry less, meditate. Anxiety is terribly aging

Learning not to worry about things I can't change

Appreciate all that I have – 'the less you want, the more you have'.

Embracing a new year

Even though it's only a date and another day, the New Year and actually, a new month or even a new week feels *different*. I'm excited at the year/month/week to come, and full of optimism of how I can better myself.

We have just been away on holiday. Our shop was closed for ten days and we were staying at a lovely, sleepy beach town a short drive from where we live. Our little poodle Atlas had a week in the country with my Poodle Rescue and retired poodle breeder friend Faye.

A beach town yes, but a beach town which has a twelve level luxurious (to us) high-rise resort/apartment building, one block from a beautiful swimming beach and with Indian and Thai restaurants, a grotty yet fun bar and various shops within a two-minute walking distance. That's my kind of beach town.

As much as I've enjoyed our end of year holiday (I typed most of this in my bikini before going for a late morning swim) my head is full of possibilities back at home.

Coming home from being away somewhere (whether it's a decent length of time or a long weekend) I am always itching to get stuck into all the little projects I am planning (and have half-finished). I think it's imperative I go away on a regular basis just so I get things done!

My focus this year is *organisation*. By being more organised at home I can be more:

Serene

Relaxed

Slimmer

Calmer

Happier

I started decluttering within the last two years, and have gained a lot, but clutter creeps up on you doesn't it? My husband calls it recluttering when I come home from the Salvation Army charity store with a new candle, rustic basket or book.

And having my fortieth birthday in October and then Christmas - both times in which I've been given lovely gifts of course. Well, our small home is now bursting at the seams. I know, it's a very Western society problem to have when you have too many gorgeous things and can't move for them.

I am full of the possibilities of making our home very similar to the luxury high-rise apartment we stayed at the beach in. From the nature of holiday accommodation it isn't filled with the 'stuff' we have in our homes. It even has floor length white gauzy curtains which blow softly in the breeze, a la my ideal French girl Sabine's Paris apartment.

And of course I have Edith Piaf playing in the background while I dream of our sparsely furnished home where every cupboard and drawer is neat and organised.

This year I will have a 'Slim Pantry' like Anne Barone's. I have streamlined it fairly recently, but you can't do it once, it needs ongoing maintenance to straighten out and find unused items which can be incorporated into a meal.

I will also have a wardrobe tidy, in which I will divide into three sections:

1. Clothing which looks **fabulous** and is **comfortable** on me right now.

2. Clothing which I **love** but is maybe a little... **snug**... to be put away and tried on at a later date.

3. Clothing which looks **frumpy** and plain on me **at any weight** and/or is a **scratchy** fabric. This clothing is being boxed up and shipped out.

Over the coming months I will be visiting every cupboard, drawer and storage hidey-hole. I will be refining my possessions and using up what I've got, before going out to any store. I will be examining how I spend my time, and how I think.

Even though I could move right into a French-style decorated home, and have a number of gilt-type pieces around the house now, I am inspired most by simple, plain and airy homes like Tara Dennis shows. I have her book 'Home – Classic Essentials for Easy Living'. I will keep it to hand to remind me what I am aiming for.

I will not decide when I've made a small improvement that that is enough. As a procrastinator and a perfectionist I have to be bold and trust that I know best!

Dreaming up the ideal life

I am back at work now after a petite Christmas holiday. It's lovely and warm here in New Zealand and summer is definitely showing her sun-kissed face.

Since we went all out for our Hawaii trip last Christmas, we kept it a bit more budget-friendly and close to home this year. My darling and I embarked on a road trip that took us to

Havelock North in Hawke's Bay where I grew up, then down to the city of Wellington for a few nights and finally we stopped in Martinborough, a bijou wine-growing district. Our entire trip was around 2,000km/1,250 miles and our final day we did almost 700km/435 miles! I haven't driven that far in a long time (well, been a passenger that far in a long time).

Despite the travel, our holiday was extremely relaxing and I read a few good books (including A Paris Apartment by Michelle Gable, which I did not want to end). I did get out of routine a little though. How can you not when you are away from home and doing different things and staying in different towns.

I enjoyed the walks I took but admit I did rather over-indulge in treat foods. Oh well, you have to do it every now and again to re-remember that yes, it might seem fun at the time but no, you still feel as unwell afterwards as you did the other times you did it…

Whilst I was out on one of my walks I got to thinking about life. What I thought about is that we spend most of our time working in a job, saving up money and paying off a house (if we're lucky), so we can sit back in retirement and enjoy our hard work. That's if we are still alive or in good enough physical shape to take advantage of our free time.

Yes, we all work hard (whether it's paid employment or not) and hope there is a payoff at the end of all that work, but that creates all the more reason to enjoy ourselves during our working life and not save up all the fun for 'one day'.

So I began to think of all the things I dream of doing one day when I'm retired and have all the time and money in the world (wouldn't that be nice) and use them for inspiration to live well *right now*. Here is my *Retirement Chic* inspiration:

The retirement me will be **fit, slim and healthy** because I have been committed to a lifestyle of nutritious food and regular exercise for a long time.

I might even have **a light tan** from daily potterings in our garden. Because the retirement me will be doing things such as weeding small areas at a time and tidying plants as I see them, we can enjoy park-like surrounds (that might be stretching it but it's nice to have a goal) on a daily basis. When I'm out walking it is so obvious the cared-for homes and gardens. It's not necessarily lots of money, but 'little and often' time spent on maintenance.

I also imagine our home being **clean, tidy and organised**. We will live in a place that is just the right size for us, and, I hope it is rural. In Martinborough we stayed in a tiny one-room cottage and it was so peaceful with no neighbours nearby, and a big open sky.

Naturally my retirement wardrobe will be a user-friendly and **stylish collection of clothing** in colours and shapes that flatter me, as I will have honed my style over the years. I think I am closing in on that style now actually, although I did the amateur's mistake of taking way too much with me on our trip. I did the same in Hawaii. That really is a skill I have to learn, but I go away so infrequently so can I use that as an excuse?

The ideal/dream/retirement me is **a writer**. How can I make that a reality? By writing daily and seeing how I can progress that.

So that's my vision of retirement, but really, what is stopping me from having and doing all these things right now? Of course I have the small thing called 'working in a shop five days a week' but surely I can work around this and make, as

Tonya Leigh says *'the journey to the dream as beautiful as the dream itself'*.

It just takes a little dreaming and planning.

Chapter 2.
Nurturing yourself

Whenever I feel tired out and like I have nothing left to give, it is because I have not been nurturing myself. Small things like going to bed at a decent hour, nourishing myself with good food and fresh water, and speaking as kindly to myself as I would a loved one go a long way to feeling fabulous.

Thankfully, just as quickly as you realise what you haven't been doing for yourself (because no-one else is going to do it if you don't), you can start those things again. Yes they might feel indulgent at first, but there's no glory in martyrdom.

Boudoir time

Anne Barone of the fabulous Chic & Slim book series mentions that chic French women take regular 'boudoir time'. This means withdrawing to their boudoir to take stock, recharge, and have quiet time alone.

My version of boudoir time is to go up to our bedroom after dinner but before bedtime. The bed is made and tidy, with pillows and cushions arranged in a pleasing way. All laundry is in the hamper, and clean clothes are hung up and put away.

I turn the bedside lamps on so there is a soft glow rather than the overhead light and spend thirty to sixty minutes or even longer reading. Often on my stomach or on my side laid out across the whole bed with either an old Victoria magazine (the French issues please) or some printed out internet inspiration (French Chic/Simplicity/Gentle Living etc) bound in a clear-file folder.

A glass of water or herbal tea is on the bedside table. Sometimes I will have a facial mask on, sometimes not, just a freshly washed face with night cream soaking in. I also massage a thick cream into neck and décolletage, hands and feet. A one-minute per foot self-massage is so dreamy and the cream helps keep your feet soft too.

As you can imagine, this time is a very relaxing prelude to drifting off to sleep. I really miss it when I don't make the time so I try to do it as often as possible. Even a mini-version is better than nothing. It's sort of a transitional time between being awake and asleep.

Quiet time

I've been having quiet time lately.

Hardly any computer at home, lots of reading, sparkling water instead of wine, home-cooking and early nights. It feels wonderful and is just what I need. Quiet time counter-balances the manic-ness that is life in our shop. Trying to keep on top of everything is a nightmare at the moment.

But I do my best and know that when we step in the door at home, it's quiet time. I take the original idea of quiet time from school-children, where the teacher designates a time to slow down, be still and relax. Soft music may be playing to assist. Quiet pursuits like reading are encouraged.

Quiet time is good for the soul, and helps you rejuvenate to face the world again.

Blissful.

Low-stress secrets

I read a great article in the December 2010 Australian Women's Weekly. '*Real-life secrets of low-stress women*' had the following tips, which I really found helpful. The bolded titles are from the article, and I have mostly paraphrased the information as well as adding my own thoughts.

Think friendly. Listen to your thoughts. Are they often negative? Do you speak to yourself in a way you wouldn't speak to a friend? I think negative thinking can be a habit we fall into, so when I catch myself I find it useful to think the positive opposite and I instantly start going in the right direction again.

Worry daily. Rather than spend all day (and night) worrying, write the worries down, and make a note of any action that could be taken. I find I do a less chic version of this. I stew and stew and let things get on top of me. Then I have a mini-breakdown and burden my husband with my woes. He makes sensible suggestions on how I can fit everything into my schedule (and never says unhelpful comments such as 'don't read blogs at work'), we make a plan and I'm happy again. Perhaps I could follow this advice, write my worries down and save him the stress.

Be grateful. Whatever you put your attention on expands and grows in your life. I've done the gratitude journal thing on and off for years since I first heard of it. I felt like a bit of a winner writing it down and thought imagine if someone read my lame writings, but I often say thank you to the

Universe for lovely things or good luck. I also often think how lucky I am to have all that I do.

Eat chocolate. Dark chocolate is good for you. I know this because I can have it in the house without eating the entire block at once. That always means things are good for you. Popcorn, icecream, jubes and milk chocolate are not good for me. I can only eat 1-2 squares of dark chocolate a day, which I cannot say for popcorn, icecream, jubes and milk chocolate. Therefore dark chocolate lives at my place while those others do not.

Take up yoga. I've already done this! I joined a class in the middle of last year. I started off going once a week and a few months in I upped it to twice a week. I had a break over Christmas of almost a month because the teacher was on holiday and I really missed it. I started back this week and I feel so good both during and after the class. I'm excited about an exercise that I enjoy and can see myself doing for the rest of my life. The magazine article said along with the facts that we know, like yoga increasing flexibility and toning muscles whilst calming the mind, is that yoga increases GABA, a brain substance which is often low in those who suffer from stress and anxiety.

Be honest. For most people lying is stressful, which is why lie detectors generally work. I heard a really cool quote recently that said 'sunshine is the best disinfectant' which I took to mean be honest, don't hide anything, and you'll feel better, healthier, happier. If you're worrying about what to say, just tell the truth.

Fall in love. The article stated that being married or in a long-term relationship alters hormones in a way that eases stress. I'm not sure that this belongs in my ideal list of low-stress secrets. Of course being in the right relationship is going to make you happier. But if you're with someone that isn't right, that can be worse than being single. And if you're single, you might feel you're missing out on a low-stress secret, when it's simply out of your control for now. You can work on yourself and be open and approachable, but it's not up to you when you meet your most excellent match. The Universe decides that. Let's kick this tip out of the list, it's too stressful. Let's go with things we can control.

Say hello to nature. This I agree with a lot. Years ago I replaced the gym with walking. I loved being outside amongst nature (even in town there are trees and gardens) more than I loved standing on carpet within walls, close to other people with loud bass music. Also, since adopting Atlas the elderly poodle, either my husband or I take five minutes every couple of hours to take a brief stroll along the grass verge. Little doses of vitamin D throughout the day! We also go for short-ish walks most days (about twenty minutes) to stretch his legs. Yesterday morning we had half an hour before we had to open the shop. Sometimes we go to a nearby cafe for a coffee (a real treat we do maybe once a week) but yesterday we walked through a nearby park. It was a lovely way to start the day.

Ask for help. Women have a tendency to try and shoulder the entire load and many of us are reluctant to ask for help. The article suggests we pick an area of our life where we could use the most help, ask the person or people we would like a helping hand from, and leave them to it. Mistakes will be made but that's part of handing over. Whenever I get the offer of help from my man and I'm tempted to say 'no that's ok I'll do it' I try and remember to say 'thank you' instead.

Eat foods rich in magnesium. I was told years ago that magnesium relaxes your muscles and helps you feel less tense. Naturally I went out and bought a magnesium supplement, which is fine, but you can also eat foods such as pumpkin seeds, brazil nuts, almonds and cashews as well as green vegetables. Another way to get it is take a bath with a handful of Epsom salts dissolved in it. Adding a few drops of lavender oil is recommended too. I'm not a fan of baths, but I do love nuts. I'll just have to remind myself to have them raw. Roasted and salted doesn't do their nutrition content any favours.

I would add to this list:

Be organised. Working on being more organised in my daily life and dealing with annoyances of my own making (such as leaving mending undone or ignoring a clutter hotspot) has made me feel infinitely happy, calm, serene and in control. Instead of walking past something twenty times before putting it away, I try and do it immediately. I'm also working on decluttering, creating good daily routines and home organisation. If I can find a place for everything and remember to put everything in its place, I will be one happy person.

Go to bed earlier. Only good things can come from this. I'm out of the habit of early nights at the moment and the times when I force myself to shut down the computer and wind down with a book before turning the light off nice and early I feel amazing the next day. My goal is for early nights to be the norm rather than the exception.

Breathe. Do you forget to breathe? I do. I find myself not exactly holding my breath, but I'm holding onto something. To lower stress, let your breath flow in... and out. And when you breathe, your stomach should expand not your chest. I think as females we are so used to holding our stomach in that we train ourselves to breathe in a counter-productive way.

Live within your means. 'Annual income twenty pounds, annual expenditure nineteen six, result happiness. Annual income twenty pounds, annual expenditure twenty pound ought and six, result misery'. - Charles Dickens. I know first-hand how horrible it feels to spend more than you have and then dread the credit card statement. It is such a good feeling to know you have money in the bank to cover your bills, plus an emergency fund of X months of living expenses (start with one month and work your way up to six to nine months seems to be the advice given by financial professionals).

How to feel better

After our dear rescue-poodle Atlas died (aged fifteen, excellent effort little fellow), I felt quite down, and this carried on to a general flatness and loss of interest in things that usually excite me. I also felt a little burnt out and detached from others.

I've never had proper depression but from time to time, right back to my teens I have had the occasional bout of mild melancholia. It's also mid-winter here so that may have something to do with it, even though I normally love the cosiness of winter.

I know it will pass with time, but meanwhile I've been doing the following to help it on its way.

Being gentle with myself, not doing too much if I don't want to. Rather than a whirlwind marathon housework day (which I just don't have the energy for at the moment) I do the basics and spend some time pottering, sewing, reading and relaxing.

Having early nights. I start winding down about 9pm and am in bed reading well before 10pm lights out. I've been sleeping like a log thank goodness. I also find I feel worse in the evening, so it's nice to wash my face good and early and hop into bed. I think my body needs lots of good, pure rest. One night last week I made noises about heading off to bed. 'But it's only ten past eight!' my husband said incredulously. That was quite funny. I managed to last until nine.

Not medicating with food and drink. When I did decide to let loose with food and drink, I felt a lot worse. Being in control of my diet and my weight goes a long way towards feeling happier.

Remembering to breathe. Often I find myself holding onto my breath. It feels such a relief to let it flow in, and out. I need to remind myself many times a day.

Keeping to my daily routines.

Talking to someone. I told my husband last night I was feeling low. I feel better for having shared it, he had some helpful suggestions, and now he is looking out for me too.

Yoga twice a week. I have missed it a few times lately and have been only attending once a week. I'm sure this has not helped my low mood as I always feel great - energised, relaxed and positive after a yoga workout.

Walking outside. I walk to yoga and back, and I also like to do errand walks on foot as long as it's not pouring with rain. A light sprinkle is ok, I take an umbrella. I met two old colleagues for lunch one day last week, and walked to meet them. It was the next suburb over and took about 45-50 minutes each way but it meant I didn't have to find a park, and got some exercise and fresh air at the same time. It was inner-city too so quite interesting.

Reading. I have been alternating my positive thinking books with pure escapism (currently the first Sophie Kinsella Shopaholic book – that series had me laughing out loud they are so crazy).

Also **escapism tv/movies.** Nothing gritty or real for me I'm afraid (now or at any other time). Keeping up with the Kardashians and the Real Housewives of Beverly Hills are great medicine I find. Not hours on end though. Just an episode here and there. I also like to re-watch favourite feel-good fun movies at times like this.

Clearing out clutter corners at home and at work. If an area is bothering me, even if I have other things to do, I attack the clutter corner. It often only takes a small amount of time, and I feel infinitely better and more able to tackle the harder jobs instantly. I went through all my trays at work on Saturday, filing and throwing out. A clear in-tray is a thing of beauty isn't it? Even if it doesn't last very long, but I *will* keep on top of it.

Taking vitamin C. I go through phases of taking vitamins, and at the moment I don't take any, but I always have vitamin C in the cupboard for when a cold threatens to come on. I read in a model beauty book ages ago that models take a 2000mg dose of vitamin C to give them a boost. As shallow as I am, I have been taking the models advice.

Be selfish and **say no.** No to library books that don't hold my attention, no to tv programmes or movies I have taped and decided I don't like. It feels hard to do, and I don't like to let people down, but learning to say no is so beneficial to our mental health. If I get a niggling feeling in my stomach when I think about something, I have been making a decision there and then to do something about it properly (not just putting it off).

Indulging in the little luxuries. I use all my lovely things and don't feel guilty at all.

Don't go shopping! No good purchasing decisions could possibly be made so I've been staying away from the shops.

Daydream about the future. I do this both by myself by writing down lists of my ideal lifestyle, home, personal style, person I want to be, and with my husband about what type of home we want to purchase, what we would do with tons of money if we won the lottery (not that we take out tickets, but still, it's fun).

Plan ahead little treats. We are booked into our favourite five-star luxury hotel right here in the city we live in a month or so's time. Just for a night. They always have good package deals and it's a mini-break we can still have while running a seven-days-a-week business. Looking forward to going really is half the fun.

Actually, I'm starting to feel a little bit better already. Have I missed anything off the list? What makes you feel better when you're low? I wonder what a chic French woman would do to combat malaise?

Recipe for a good night's sleep

We have finally employed someone apart from my husband and myself in the shop. She is wonderful and with us three days a week, but it still seems like I am always catching my tail.

Yesterday I had a day off at home to bless our abode with cleanliness and order. Looking forward to a day such as this, where I go nowhere and see no one (except for our rescue-cat Miss Jessica, who is my little shadow), makes me realise how much I love living a routine and simple life.

When life gets hectic, I realise I invariably end up going to bed too late. Often it is not from doing a job which needs to be done, but just because I am fluffing around. Perhaps if I feel rushed and busy, going to bed early makes me feel guilty because there is something else I could be doing?

I like to make a conscious effort to take these steps in order to have a good rest and wake refreshed the next day.

- Early dinner (served around seven is early for us), one glass of wine maximum, or sparkling mineral water

- Computer turned off before dinner/no computer after dinner or at least 1 hour before bedtime (not only does the lit screen wake up my brain, but I find myself click-click-clicking my time away)

- Take plenty of time for my bathroom routine – makeup removal, cleansing and moisturising, brush and floss teeth.

- Read after dinner instead of the computer or tv, with a cup of tea and lights out well before ten pm.

Chapter 3.
Living a life of style

Call me shallow, but I do love thinking about the concept of living a life of luxurious style. I don't necessarily want to spend a lot of money, and I'm always looking around for inspiration on how to elevate my life (while still keeping the simplicity that I crave) to one of high style on a minimal budget.

Living a chic life

With my interest in all things chic, how could I pass up a book entitled 'Chic - life as it should be'. Stylish and authoritative. One reviewer said the author Colin Cowie made Martha Stewart look like a slob, and reading this book confirms that as a fact. Apart from writing books, he is a very highbrow events co-ordinator.

It is a very inspiring read, and makes me get up and declutter a shelf after finishing a chapter. For example, rather than have a bedside table cluttered with everything you could ever want to reach for, Colin has the top drawer all but empty, with the essentials laid out on one of those lacy thin rubber mats cut to fit the drawer (to stop everything sliding around).

For me, body butter, hand cream, lip cream, lip balm, pen and paper, mini alarm clock and a few other bits and pieces (like my bookmark collection so I always have a pretty one to use). And then you would have a few choice items on the top. He said his goal is to have his home look like a chic hotel.

This book also has many pictures of Colin's home in NYC. His style is a little masculine for me, however I can appreciate the stylish orderliness and I covet his labelled, stacked, grouped closets and cupboards.

Here is a wonderfully motivating excerpt from the book:

The foundation of any well-run home is cleanliness and order. An orderly house will not only give you pleasure, it will also make everything in your life, from writing a thank-you note the day after a fabulous evening to opening your home to over-night guests, that much more effortless.

Living elegantly means creating a place you look forward to coming home to, a place where you can entertain happily, harmoniously, and generously.

If my home is in order, I feel as though my life is in order and I can take on anything. I love walking into an intelligently designed, immaculate kitchen. I love opening the freezer door and finding everything I need neatly stacked: frozen appetisers ready to be popped into the oven, decorator ice cubes available to enliven a chic cocktail, chicken stock waiting to form the base of a delicious home-made soup.

In the closet, I love finding my shirts arranged from light to dark, short-sleeve to long, beautifully starched, and hanging from matching hangers. I love clean, polished surfaces that are stripped of any unnecessary clutter. I love opening my desk drawers and immediately finding business cards, personal stationery, pens, and my cell phone charger. And at night, I love retiring to a bedroom so pulled together and luxuriously welcoming that I could easily mistake it for a five star hotel suite.

Keep the things that are precious to you close by and available so they can be used on a regular basis. Everything else should be stored in a safe place, not left out on display. Serving bowls should be on the tables only when they're overflowing with food, and there's nothing at all exciting about an empty vase perched on a windowsill (even if it's Lalique!). Less is definitely more!

For example, a simple vase with one exotic flower on a central table can be more astonishing than that same vignette surrounded by fourteen framed pictures and half a dozen objets from your last European vacation.

Instead, keep a separate closet or cupboard where you can store your collection of decorative items. When you bring them out for entertaining, they'll seem brand new again. Use your pieces to create varied and interesting vignettes and fresh atmospheres, then put them away for the next time the mood strikes.

Invest in drawer dividers, baskets, and closet organisers. Trays and decorative bowls can also be fantastic containers for odds and ends such as keys and loose change. Create areas for everything you use, which will allow you to find what you're looking for when you're looking for it.

Try to take twenty minutes each day to tidy up and put things back where they belong. When you're having a few friends over for drinks or throwing a party, you shouldn't have to do a major all-day cleaning. The longer you delay straightening up, the more burdensome it is to clean. It's much better, and a lot less overwhelming, to maintain order and cleanliness as you move through your day.

Granted, most people work and have to scramble to keep up with household chores. But ideally, you'll get to a point where with a bit of soap and water, a mop and a broom, some dimmer switches on the lights and a little music, your home should be ready to receive guests at practically a moment's notice. A little at a time goes a long way.

--

I saw Colin and his partner on Oprah and he was so engaging and funny I couldn't help but liking him. His partner said if he ever wants to upset Colin all he has to do is shake a drawer so everything gets mixed up. Colin may sound a little OCD-ish but he makes it seem so appealing.

I think Colin's advice to take a small amount of time to tidy up each day is so wise. It really makes a huge difference to both the smooth running of my household, and my levels of serenity. I also changed my bedside table to reflect Colin's recommendations two and a half years ago when I first read the book, and it is still like that today. It must be working.

Elegance is refusal

When I first heard the Coco Chanel quote *elegance is refusal*, the first thought that came to me was food. That I had to refuse food to become elegant and trim like the bird-like Mademoiselle Chanel. And being a food-lover there was no way I could picture myself eating tiny portions so I've always had a bit of a block towards these words.

Lately and from two different sources I have heard of a more enticing way to look at it, which ties in perfectly with my love of curating a beautiful life by decluttering items that do not fit the vision of the lifestyle I have for myself.

And that is just it – refusal of anything that does not elevate your life to exquisite elegance.

Refusing junky foods in favour of high quality fresh foods.

Refusing possessions that detract from rather than add to my enjoyment of life. And this includes refusal of excess possessions. We all like different ways of living, but I feel at my most content when I have less around me.

Refusing clothing that does not make me look and feel chic and sophisticated. That includes clothing I wear to work or out, loungewear at home, nightwear and lingerie. Everything!

Refusing to be around people that bring me down or make me feel bad about myself.

Refusing to accept others beliefs as gospel. I'm cultivating my own wonderful and empowering beliefs thank you very much.

Refusing negative thoughts because they don't feel good *and* they weaken your immune system. Apparently it's been proven in tests which gave me a jolt when I heard that.

Refusing to listen to myself when I say something is too big or scary to entertain. What could I achieve if I believed I could do that huge achievement. Why would I block it from my mind immediately? Even if I never do it, I've at least not closed my mind to it.

Chapter 4.
Chic habits

It is the little things that you do on a daily basis that are so important, because these are the moments that make up your life. There is no one big thing we are waiting for, believe it or not, and it's the habitual way we live our lives that gives it its flavour.

Switch unhelpful habits out for habits that improve your life and watch how you suddenly start heading in the direction you desire. It's as simple as that!

Go to bed earlier, get up earlier

For the past several years, I have been getting up an hour earlier, all so I can drink hot tea with milk and read – usually blogs, less often a book or magazine. I can have a lovely time catching up on all my favourite blogs and do my own writing. It's now routine for me to get up earlier and I absolutely love this time.

In the height of summer when I started doing this it was lovely and light already, but as we creep towards Autumn it's a little dark at first (I get up around 6-6.30am, not that early compared to a lot of folk. Our shop doesn't open until 9.30am so we often leave for work around 9am) but I still enjoy this early time, even if the blinds are still down and the lights are on for the first part.

It's guilt free time too. I know it's not good to surf the net when at work – there are important things to do there, and being self-employed I'm not doing myself any favours. And in the evenings I feel like a terrible wife glued to the laptop screen while my husband is sitting by himself on the sofa. So I get my fix first thing. And I've restarted my 'book', you know, the book we're all writing. I feel like a bit of a fraud writing, I don't know why. But I love reading so much and I have told myself – even if no one else reads it. Write a book you would like to read.

One I just finished and which I enjoyed immensely is A Spring Affair by Milly Johnson. I do love chick lit to relax and escape – there is so much uninspiring formulaic stuff out there though that it's exciting to find a new author. Some I love are Sophie Kinsella (all of them), Emily Giffin (all of them) and Emily Barr (have only read Plan B but loved it – and it had a French angle).

I picked up A Spring Affair from the library new releases shelf and upon reading the back cover found it was, ta da, a new genre 'decluttering chick lit'. Imagine! I had to borrow it of course and found it was such a lovely, funny, enjoyable book which actually had me in tears over my breakfast at the end. I love those books! And it had decluttering advice all the way through. A book tailor made for me I think. And maybe you too if you're a chick lit fan and as obsessed with decluttering as I am.

I went to the author's website after I had finished and apart from a section on decluttering (yay), found tips for budding authors. If nothing else, she said, write 250 words per day, no matter what, and at the end of the year you will have a 91,000 word book. And don't edit, just keep writing. Edit right at the end otherwise you will lose momentum. So that's what I'm doing in the morning now. Before I start anything else, I write at least 250 words and then I am free to read all those inspiring blog posts.

So I can heartily recommend going to bed earlier and getting up earlier. After all, what do you do in the last hour of the evening anyway, lie there on the sofa thinking I'm too tired to get up and wash my face, watching tv that isn't even any good, nothing actually productive. Sometimes I do that exact thing and go to bed at 11pm. That's only 7 hours sleep – not nearly enough! I like to start getting ready for bed around nine and be in bed reading by 9.30-10. I aim for nine hours sleep like apparently French women get, but eight is a good minimum.

How to stay young

I wish there was a tape recorder going for the conversation I had with this customer, because I don't think anyone will believe me when I relay it to them.

A nice, well-dressed lady was buying a pair of shoes, and said she needed them to get around in the weekend and watch the grandchildren play rugby on a Saturday morning.

'Grandkids!' I spluttered. 'You look too youthful to have grandkids, what's your secret?' I asked her. After I said it I realised it may be misconstrued as an impolite question (starting very young etc). Luckily she didn't take offence.

'What cream do you use?' I quizzed. 'None really', she said 'I don't use much at all.' 'Good genes?' I asked again. 'No, that's not it. My mother has a lot of age spots'.

After a bit she said 'Sex! Lots of sex. I'm not joking. Have sex. And have it a lot.'

Cue my startled face and then an interesting conversation. I'm no prude but she was very upfront and happy to tell me her secret to defying her age. And ten minutes before I'd never met her.

I told her about an Oprah show I saw a while back about a couple who were overweight, tired out and unhappy. They decided to rev up their life by making a pact to have sex every day for a year. You can imagine how vibrant, trim and healthy this couple looked after the year was up, not to mention happy and smiling, with an enviable energy.

'It would be hard if you were single though' I put to her. 'Oh, my friends think I'm terrible' she said, 'but I have a 'friend' who's ten years younger than me and we've been getting together for a couple of years. I've had marriage and I've had long term relationships, I just can't be bothered with those now. I'm happy being single and just getting together with my friend every so often.'

I admit I was a little speechless (and impressed with her candour) at this stage. She recommended sex as the best exercise you can have, and of course it is fun and free.

Just in case you are wondering otherwise, she wasn't tacky or tarty looking. She just looked like a pleasant, normal woman who might be standing in front of you at the supermarket checkout. Except that you might think she was 45 when she was really 55. I didn't have the cheek to ask her age, but I was dying to know.

She asked if I always worked Fridays and I said I did, as she wanted to come in again for another pair of shoes and would come when I was there. Maybe I'll find out then.

Swapping stockpiling for tranquility

I know this is such a 'first world problem' to have, but in our Western culture of stocking up, stockpiling and overstocking, there is something very satisfying of *having just enough*.

I used to love stockpiling bargains on consumables such as pantry food items and toiletries. But now in an effort to live more simply and have less noise around me, I've tempered my ways.

I'm embarrassed to say there have been times when I've gone overboard and it has taken us months to plough through whatever specially-priced item I stocked up on.

Our big box supermarkets often have enticements to 'spend $200 and receive a petrol discount voucher' which has regularly encouraged us to see what we need and stock up on it. But in a household of two people and two cats, we really have to try hard to spend $200 in one go. It was quite stressful just to gain a coupon that saved us about $10-12 (which isn't to be scoffed at, I agree, but not worth it if you are crowded out of your house with grocery items that might not be used for many months, if at all!)

So I gave myself permission not to stockpile. I gave myself permission to let something run out and see if I missed it. Sometimes I did and sometimes I didn't. It is quite a lovely feeling to see space in the pantry and see what items I can use up to make a delicious dinner.

It is also refreshing to know that I can use up my many skincare and cosmetic items before I even need to think of perusing another specials brochure. *I don't even need to look at that brochure because I already have enough skin cream/shampoo/body lotion.*

Speaking of body lotion, a couple of months ago I bought a 5 litre (1 1/3 gallons!) container of body lotion from a local skincare factory shop, how funny is that. But I do go through it is vast quantities.

It's quite fun to see how many days we can *not* go to the supermarket, and if we need something, it's put on the shopping list for when we really, really need to go.

We often pop into fruit and vegetable stores to get fresh produce, but the supermarket list can wait for quite a number of days until we have to go. And it still might only be less than a dozen items. It's such a thrill not to have armfuls of grocery bags to bring into the house. Plus, there is not money coming out of my wallet while I'm doing this.

When you think about it, I must live a pretty sheltered life if *not stockpiling* is acting in a risky way, so I feel very lucky about that. Many people in other parts of the world would *wish* this was their most pressing concern.

Are you a stockpiler? Bargain hunter extraordinaire? Does the thought of having space on your bathroom/kitchen/laundry shelves make you nervous? 'Not-stockpiling'. It's the new way to save time, sanity and money don't you know.

Cultivating calmness

'Make inner peace your highest goal and you will probably never make another mistake.' – Brian Tracy

I heard this listening to an audiobook by my friend Brian Tracy when I was driving home from work a few days ago. I wrote it down at the next red light and put it in my little French Chic notebook when I got home. I have been repeating it to myself since I first heard it and it has been so helpful and comforting.

Getting worked up over little things always makes me feel awful and I know it's not good for me, both mentally and physically. Now that I have taken on board to 'make inner peace my highest goal', situations that I would have become quite annoyed with were simply smoothed over and I felt much better about everything afterwards even though 'by rights' I should have been bothered about something.

In an instance where I feel myself becoming peeved over a minor annoyance, I repeat the saying to myself and instantly feel transformed. Inner peace is a wonderful thing to strive for and I'm going to use Brian's saying almost as my life motto.

I was at the supermarket just before, and I noticed I was overcharged for two items. I went to the customer services desk and was told I was wrong. I was sure I was right but after querying them a bit more and them telling me I could ring the toll-free number for their head office to check it out, I said I trusted them, and left the store.

I had planned to call the head office once I got to the car 'for my own peace of mind' to know if I was incorrect or they were. By the time I opened my car door I had been repeating my new mantra to myself and realised it wasn't worth the $1.89 difference to me (even though I believe the saying that if you look after the pennies the pounds will look after themselves).

I could see me spending time on hold and getting myself all churned up talking to someone trying to prove I was right. It wasn't worth it! Making inner peace my highest goal saved the day and I was calm as I drove home.

I read about Kim Cattrell in an English magazine (Woman & Home, May 2013). She was being interviewed, among other things, about how incredible she looks for her age. This is what she said:

When I hit my forties I thought, 'I can't play a sexy siren anymore.' Almost 20 years later, it's still going on. I think that's because I take care of myself, which includes dieting, exercising and minimizing stress.

I joke that I've been on a diet since 1974, which is basically true. I like to eat, and my body type is not naturally this thin, especially at this age. So I do watch what I eat and drink but I'm not obsessive – it's just a way of life. So I don't have dessert after every meal – I just can't do it.

I have a big appetite, and staying on top of that is about knowing myself and saying, 'I can eat that today but tomorrow I'm not going to.' And I'm always aware – from gaining and losing weight for parts – that the time in the gym trying to lose extra weight is really hard work! I always have that in my mind.

Apart from the fact that I was impressed with her honesty, I thought it was so interesting that she included reducing stress in her life as one of her keys to staying slim, healthy and youthful-looking.

You often hear celebrities talk about meditation and I even bought myself Meditation for Dummies which actually is a wonderful book. But I still would get all righteous and worked up over small injustices in daily life and the meditation book couldn't fix that.

I always felt like I wanted everything to be fair. It was easy when I was the one who had to tell the truth, give back the wallet I found with $400 in it, own up to a mistake and all those sorts of things. But when it's the other person who should be 'giving in', well, you can't control that and it's stressful when you try!

So as good as my meditation book was, it didn't help me be calm in various situations. My 'new life motto' does. It helps me see the truth and live a peaceful life. It applies to any and every situation that I have tested it on so far and I am very thankful that I came across it.

Chapter 5.
Inspiration on living well

If you've ever lacked *motivation* to do something that you desperately want to achieve and can't quite get there, why not try it from the other way – use *inspiration* to help you get what you want. It's pulling you towards something rather than you trying to push yourself, and is far more effective. Save your energy for where it is needed elsewhere!

Following are my favourite petite essays inspired by the thought of living well. We each have our own idealistic lifestyle – these show you mine. I hope they will be helpful in your journey of refining how you want your life to look and feel.

Living a small life

The more time I spend on this earth, the more I realise I can please myself and be myself. I don't need to pretend to want great things and I don't need to fret that I've never had or probably never will have a high-powered career.

I've come to realise that's not what I'm about. I enjoy a quiet and simple life. Ever since I left school I've always worked at 'normal' office jobs. I didn't attend University because I didn't really know what I wanted to study, and I didn't want to go just for the sake of it. So I started my first full-time job at eighteen (although I had already been working part-time after school and in school holidays since I was fourteen) and have been working ever since.

My husband and I now own a small retail business which we started almost seven years ago. We have decided for now we are content with one shop and a simple online presence. We've talked about it and agreed that opening a second or subsequent shops wouldn't necessarily make us any happier.

It's all about balance. By running one shop between us we have the flexibility during the day to do things such as run errands, go to the gym or yoga, take a walk, or just disappear for a while if we want to.

In terms of a social life, I've had my times of going out a lot especially when single. But even then I loved nothing more than to be at home with the fire lit, knitting or reading. I knew I had to go out to meet someone though for they don't come knocking at your door, so I did what I had to (and actually met the perfect man for me, now my husband, in a bar).

It's not just about what I do for a job, or socialising though, it's everything in my life. I happily share one very ordinary car and enjoy creative and frugal pursuits at home. Expensive hobbies scare me.

Even though I enjoy the dream of living in or travelling to Paris or New York City, I love living in New Zealand and can't see myself living anywhere else. And for travel, I know it will come, I'm happy to forego it now, in this phase of my life where we are running a business.

If it sounds like I'm putting off happiness, I'm not. Every day I feel grateful and satisfied and thankful that I am where I am.

I enjoy small luxuries frequently and make my own happiness. I collect simple pleasures such as going to bed early.

My Mum always said 'bored people are boring' when we complained of having nothing to do. I guess I took that to heart as now there aren't enough hours in the day for all the things I love to do – reading, writing, sewing, knitting, cooking, pottering, movie-watching – as well as living my everyday life in a thoughtful and stylish manner.

I no longer feel I have to apologise for not being a faster and more driven person. I am content to live my own life, at my own pace.

That's the greatest luxury of all I think: living a life custom-designed for me.

Living as our grandparents did

I've never really thought of myself as 'green', more 'old-fashioned'. But the more I research, the more I'm convinced they are almost the same thing. Our ancestors went about life in a thrifty and non-wasteful way. Meals were made from scratch, clothing was made and then mended, nothing was wasted and people read books for entertainment. This wasn't just a quaint notion, there really was no other alternative to all these things.

In my generation we went away from this in favour of conspicuous consumption. Thank goodness thrift is back in vogue again. Plus we have all this wonderful technology, so we really are lucky enough to have the benefit of both worlds.

Aside from the saving money aspect, I feel disrespectful if I waste food, or throw away something that could have been used by someone else. In fact I just can't do it. When we were moving house I drove my husband nuts, sifting through everything we were decluttering, figuring out where it could be donated to.

As much as I love those decluttering programmes on tv, it really upsets me to have the solution be a big skip outside, where everything is thrown in. If an item is in good, usable, clean, unbroken condition there is always someone who could use it that otherwise might not have the chance. I think it is our duty as a caring human being to try and find that person, via thrift shops, to charities that assist others or simply directly, by asking around.

Other ways I am like our grandparents?

I scrubbed our kitchen floor and entrance-way with hot water and sugar soap not long after we moved in (it was pretty filthy). Strongly-scented floor cleaners aren't for me. Normally I use hot water, white vinegar and a squirt of lemon dishwash. A few drops of essential oil are added if I'm in the mood. I also hang washing outside. And cook many of our meals from scratch.

Even when eating, the question could be asked 'would my Grandparents recognise this food?' when choosing what to eat. The world's population would be a much healthier place if we ate according to this.

Many of the ways in which our grandparents lived that are now trendy were originally done in the name of thrift or making do. I do these things to make the most of my resources, and also because I feel disrespectful to the Universe if I waste things.

I simply cannot throw something in the rubbish if it can be used by someone else (so I donate it) and I feel terribly guilty if I throw out food. If it's vegetation I throw out I feel bad that the Universe grew it for me and I wasted it. Even more guilt is felt if it's meat or eggs I throw out. An animal died (or laid) for me and I can't even be bothered to appreciate it?

As a result I throw out practically nothing. I honestly can't remember the last time I threw out food. If I don't eat something as leftovers for lunch the next day (like our creamy chicken and mushroom pasta from tonight, which I'll have with salad for lunch tomorrow), I will tuck it in the freezer to have another day. If it's something like a small piece of blue cheese or half a chopped onion, I will freeze to include in a casserole or soup.

Another aspect of living like our grandparents did is mending something if it's broken. There is much satisfaction to be gained from utilising our grey matter and working out how we can fix a problem. My sister was telling me today how she hemmed a pair of jeans shorter, and in the process used the excess denim to almost invisibly patch a hole in the knee. Result: one 'new' pair of jeans which are currently receiving a lot of wear.

I understand not everyone sews, but really, in the olden days it was just something you did. If one is really interested in living a thrifty life, at least knowing how to sew on buttons, hand-stitch a hem or sew up a small hole is mandatory.

Reading instead of tv watching, going for a stroll after dinner, eating real food, being a good steward of our finances, appreciating nature, growing herbs or even vegetables, making things with our hands: these are all ways we can enjoy life by living as our grandparents did.

Kaizen

I was talking with my husband about making our new (twenty three year old) home better over time, both with cleaning effort and low-cost updates. He then told me about *kaizen*, which is Japanese for *small and gradual improvement* and that's how their successful companies work.

I actually got very excited by this as it's how I live my life, and there's a name for it. How often does that happen? I don't really go for high-cost, high-maintenance but enjoy finding the do-it-yourself low-cost, creative route.

Because we are focused on paying our home loan off in a much shorter time than the standard twenty five years, we have decided to wait and see what improvements we want to do that require serious capital input.

We also practice this with our shop. I see other retail stores that spend big dollars on a fancy fitout (and make me feel like we should do the same) but within a few years have closed down.

Everything we do in our business we ask 'how many pairs of shoes do we have to sell to pay for this, and is it worth it?' Of course we have to be professional, but there are many, many ways to waste money I have found.

And we want our shop to be around for a long time. Being fiscally responsible is one way to ensure that as much as possible.

I often think imagine if you had a camera set up that took time-lapse photos of your home. It would show from the date you moved in how much better it looked month on month and year on year.

I'm sure 'kaizen' isn't a better known term (or maybe you've already heard of it) because it's not as exciting as the 'big reveal' of a makeover programme where everything is changed in an instant and everything is brand-new.

Just like a diet, slow and steady brings gradual and permanent change. As others have wisely noted in the comments section, our tastes change over time too, so if you redecorate your home all at once (obviously having just won the lottery), mightn't you get sick of it soon?

As with personal style, I think it's better to grow into your home look.

On living a low-key life

I read a book called My Friend Michael by Frank Cascio a while back, about Michael Jackson. His life sounded so glamorous being filled with first class travel, the money to buy whatever he wanted, fabulous hotels where he booked out an entire floor, not to mention being an international celebrity.

But sadly we all know how Michael's story ended. As he grew bigger and bigger he began taking prescription medicines just to cope with the stress of it all. Part of me wonders why he didn't downsize his life and just enjoy what he had, but as it was all he had known from age five, that thought probably didn't occur to him.

Besides, you don't get to be an international pop superstar by being a relaxed person who takes things in their stride.

As a side note, it was a fabulous book and I was really impressed by Michael's goal-setting and visualisation that the author described so well. The book is a good motivational tool. I made heaps of notes!

I have a cousin who, having just turned thirty is an extremely successful businessman that lives literally all over the world. He has two homes (Miami and London) and probably spends more time in hotel rooms and airplanes than he does in those.

He commented to a family member a while back that he feels sorry for me to be 'stuck' in our shop every day and never going anywhere. I was quite astounded when I heard that as I have never felt this way and don't consider our shop to be any different from other jobs I have had where I was obliged to show up at the office each day. It's just what I do.

An international life sounds glamorous and fun in theory, and I am definitely guilty of daydreaming when I see the celebrity photos of all the stars striding out from the airport gates (I have to process what they are wearing – cool sunglasses, check, leggings or skinny jeans, check, great jacket and loopy scarf, check).

But I am a home-loving person at heart who relishes routine and early nights, nesting and home-cooked meals. If I even have too many late nights I am all out of sorts.

And to do all these things that I love you have to have a job or lifestyle that means you can live in the one city and be home at a reasonable hour. I love that I spend each day in a familiar place and come to the same home each night.

When I go away on a rare holiday I just cannot wait to get home. Heck, even when I am out for the day I cannot wait to get home!

So I guess it's lucky I am not an international jetsetter then isn't it? But in the meantime I will enjoy perfecting the superstar travel uniform, just in case.

Simplicity manifesto

My idea of a minimalist has always been a free spirit who travels the world with only six items of clothing and a fancy Apple laptop in their backpack. I don't know why, it's just the image that pops into my head.

This makes me feel like a fraud when I consider myself a minimalist, but then just who decided the definition of minimalism and does it involve a certain number of possessions? Even though I know no-one decided, I do like this description from The Minimalists (and funny that they mention the same thing I did about the stereotypical minimalist). They say:

Minimalism is a tool that can assist you in finding freedom. Freedom from fear. Freedom from worry. Freedom from overwhelm. Freedom from guilt. Freedom from depression. Freedom from the trappings of the consumer culture we've built our lives around. Real freedom.

And who doesn't want more freedom I ask you?

So I've decided to create my own definition of minimalism to help guide me to my own personal happiness.

Dave Ramsey has a great quote that goes *'live like no-one else today so that you can live like no-one else tomorrow'*. I love this saying and it really makes me excited at the possibilities I have for my life. It also keeps my encouragement up for living the way I do and having my own minimalist mindset.

I love that we are paying off our home loan much earlier than the standard 20+ years because it means we have more choices in the kind of work we do and how many hours we work.

I love that I don't need much to make me happy. I'm a real home-lover and relish time spent in my abode surrounded by the things I love such as books, music and creative projects. But compared with our friends, we don't have nearly as many expensive possessions.

My minimalism manifesto could equally be called a Simplicity Manifesto because I have such a beautiful craving for simplicity and it is actually one of my core values.

In putting together my ~~Minimalism~~ Simplicity Manifesto I will involve statements big and small such as:

I am intentional with what I allow into my life, whether it is an item, an obligation or a person.

I enjoy doing the laundry because I love everything I've worn and washed, and there is ample room to put it away when it is clean, dry and folded.

I will find magic in everything I do, because I want to live a magical life.

This is an ongoing project which I am enjoying working on!

A life of luxury

The word *luxury* is such an enchanting word, and there are many different meanings you can attach to it. I love to daydream about living a luxurious life. Yes, having material luxury goods is part of that daydream, but whether I am willing to pay for them and take care of them is another matter altogether.

On the rare occasion that I purchase a lottery ticket (maybe once or twice a year), it is a fun game for my husband and myself to plan what we are going to do with our winnings. That alone is almost worth the price of the ticket. We decide what we are going to do with the shop, where we will travel to and where we will live. We talk about what our new daily routine might be.

It is at these times that I reinforce to myself that we live a life of luxury already. Yes, we have to go to work, but how I conduct myself when I'm there, and what we do at home I encourage myself to do in a way that I think I would should I win that luxurious lottery lifestyle

Fresh fruit and vegetables every day. In the morning for breakfast a bowl overflowing with any of these, fresh and sliced – pineapple, strawberries, pear, apple, apricots, orange – topped with a handful of mixed raw nuts.

For lunch a luscious salad of lettuce, both home-grown and store-bought, home-grown fresh herbs torn on top, and any or all of sliced carrots, capsicum, celery, cucumber, tomato, then finished with good protein such as a couple of hard-boiled eggs, shredded roast chicken or tuna at a pinch and always avocado. Creamy dressings are my treat - I love Paul Newman's Caesar dressing and ranch as well.

In the evening a home-cooked meal, perhaps a roast? With roast vegetables and steamed broccoli, cauliflower and asparagus dressed in extra-virgin olive oil.

And of course glass after glass of fresh, clear, life-giving water throughout the day.

Am I in a fancy health spa or a top-notch country hotel? No! This is what I eat every day at home. I have gradually increased my consumption of fresh fruit and vegetables over time so that now the majority of my diet consists of them.

I am slowly and permanently ironing out poor dietary habits and changing them to new, healthy ones. As an added bonus, being slender and feeling vibrant is on my luxury lifestyle list too.

Spa-like pampering. Soft smooth exfoliated legs and arms, polished brightly coloured toenails, blow-dried silky hair and lightly applied make-up. I don't have to visit a spa for all these things, I just need to allow plenty of time in the morning to get ready (because I like to move slowly). I also remind myself that all these pampering things don't take very long, they are virtually free, and the results are worth it (I need that reminder on lazy days sometimes).

Having a leisurely start to the day. To have plenty of time to get ready in the morning, I made the decision years ago that I would rise at 6am every day, whether it was a work day or a day at home. It's better for your body to get up at the same time every day. It doesn't have to be 6am, but that's what time I have to get up to get ready for work, so I do it on my weekends too.

If you get up at different times throughout the week you give yourself a form of jetlag. And I read recently that having greatly varying times of getting up and bedtime is worse for retaining weight, just another reason to set my alarm.

Always having an engrossing book to read, be it fiction or non-fiction. Having a rich inner life is the best way to live a luxurious life on little money, and a book is a great vehicle. I read from my current book or books every day, always with my breakfast, sometimes with my lunch, sometimes before dinner, and definitely in bed when I retire for the evening. I don't often buy a book straight away, instead I borrow from the library first and then buy new if I like it enough for my personal library at home. I also browse charity stores and can pick up great books from there. They aren't usually more than a dollar or two. Sometimes they are keepers and sometimes I read and re-donate.

Beautiful music as my personal soundtrack. I have many playlists on my iPod that I play at home depending on my mood. There are Buddha Bar/Hotel Costes/Café del Mar ones for when I want to feel cool and connected to the world, Richard Clayderman and Carl Doy for when I want to feel hotel-ish when I am doing my housework, relaxing classical adagios to feel elegant and peaceful, jazz for dinner guests or lazy Sundays and many more. Music is a must in my luxury lifestyle.

Surrounding myself with beauty and order. At home I prefer calming colours. Even something as pedestrian as a washing basket I chose white, so it would blend in in the laundry or when I am putting clothing away. I couldn't cope with a bright blue one for example. Picking up and putting away as I move around the house keeps things looking tidy and helps my serenity.

Always having space to put something away at home is luxurious to me, that is why I love decluttering so much. The satisfaction I gain from editing and organizing a space for maximum ease and future pleasure is immense!

Chic Inspiration:
Imaginative ways to live a more magical life

Chapter 6.
Favourite chic inspiration

The posts in this chapter are among my all-time favourites, and readers too, judging from my blog statistics. I love how you can read something uplifting and it switches your mindset so you end up having a better day than you might have otherwise.

What you focus on becomes more prevalent in your life, so why not focus on something beautiful?

Being feminine in everyday life

One of the things I love most about being born a girl, is the chance to indulge in the daily expression of being feminine. The ideal French woman is the ultimate in sophisticated elegance and femininity.

Here are some of my favourite ways to feel feminine every day:

I remind myself to **walker slower and more elegantly**. I imagine I am a chic woman in a movie. Channelling Amelie or another movie character is fun if I am feeling in a frump. It immediately makes you lighter on your toes and more expressive, in a non-over the top way of course.

Wearing soft, pretty colours near my face. Or softening a dark top with pearls or a scarf that throws a flattering light onto my complexion. Wearing a bright colour feels very feminine too. Not a clown of brights though, one bright colour with a neutral is my favourite way. Red with white, denim with Kelly green, black with soft blush pink/beige.

Standing up straight, imagine a string pulling me up from the crown of the head. **Imagine you are a ballet dancer** when you move.

Wear **lightly applied makeup in soft, sheer tones** that flatter my colouring. Ensure there are no hard lines and that everything is well blended.

Eat and drink in moderation. Indulge in chic foods I could **imagine a svelte Parisian woman eating**. Sometimes if I am stuck for a lunch idea I ask myself, if I lived in my bijoux Paris apartment, what would I make? And I must admit, as much as I enjoy relaxing with a tasty brandy, I always feel more feminine with a sparkling mineral water.

Doing **daily stretches and gentle exercise walks**. I do errands on foot if they are near. A tote bag is used including sunglasses, and a fold-up umbrella if the weather is inclement.

Let **not one critical word** come from my mouth, either about myself or others. This is an ongoing challenge for me. I am working on overruling negative thoughts with positive ones. And trying not to be so instantly judgemental.

Make my **thoughts positive – it softens the face**. It really is incredible how facial expressions (on a seemingly neutral face) can make you seem hard or soft.

Washing hair more frequently. Men love **clean, fresh-scented hair**, and so do I. It feels amazing.

Take an extended **bathroom spa time** on the weekend. Exfoliate thoroughly over my whole body, apply lotion, polish toe-nails.

Part of my coming home routine in the evening is to remove all jewellery. But I sometimes leave something on, ie **pearl earrings. Just to be pretty.**

Lightly spritz with a **feminine fragrance** every now and then.

Surrounding myself with feminine colours. Not just in clothing and makeup, but everything in my life – home furnishings, stationery etc. Some of my favourite colours are soft beige-pinks, creamy whites and silvers, dove grey, ethereal sea glass blue-green.

Playing **music as a background**, much like movies do. Gentle classical pieces and relaxing spa music is fabulous for having on low as I go about my day. French hotel sounds such as Buddha Bar, Six Senses and Hotel Costes are an enjoyable alternative that instantly make my everyday life seem much more cool. They are often very sexy too. And that's never a bad thing.

Having softness around me – mohair rugs in the winter or soft, cool cotton palazzo pants in the summer. One of my favourite ways to make a difference to the bed is to place a light-weight duvet inner under the sheets as a kind of mattress topper. It makes your bed feel very luxe and cloud-like. And it stays in place under the fitted sheet, even without straps or elastic. I like that I can wash it regularly too, unlike my mattress, which doesn't really fit in the machine.

Being a domestic goddess. It's true what they say about a home needing a woman's touch. As I enter or leave a room I try to do one thing to straighten or tidy. I open the windows every day, even in winter if only for an hour or two, so that our house smells airy and fresh. **Making your home a peaceful retreat** for you and your family is a very feminine thing to do.

Being 'French'

I love reading, thinking and writing about the idealistic French girl. Whether it's actually true or not really makes no difference to me. I am inspired to be a better (and better-*groomed*) person because of these ideals and that's the important thing to me.

In thinking about whether I actually put into my life what I love to daydream about, I have to ask, do I walk the talk? I'm sure there are women living in Paris who would laugh at the 'French girl' descriptions, or perhaps they really are all like the books say. So here are ways I have incorporated some French-inspired ideals into my life.

Walking. I sometimes walk purely for exercise, where I put on my running shoes, a t-shirt and a pair of knit pants and walk for an hour, briskly. Lately though I have been blending my exercise walk with errands.

Previously, I would walk for an hour, get back and then drive to the supermarket, bank, post office etc. Now, I often go out for a walk in my normal clothing, just adding a pair of comfortable walking shoes (not running shoes) and carrying a tote bag that slings over my shoulder. I can then walk to the bank, post office, shops. As long as I'm not buying too much I'm okay. Obviously for a big supermarket shop I take the car.

Natural hair and makeup. I have always worn makeup, however now I wear less. I want a subtle glow, and long, dark lashes. I use a sheer, water-based foundation and use a very light hand with powder, blush, lipstick, eyebrow pencil, eye shadow, eyeliner and mascara. Often on a day at home when I wear just tinted moisturiser and even smaller amounts of the above I think how pretty the effect is. So as time goes on I can see myself wearing less and less - but always some.

With my hair, I had it my natural colour for many years (medium blonde), but now with greys creeping in it has started looking a little... drab. Bearing in mind advice not to stray too far from your natural colour, I have been having blonde highlights and my own colour lowlights together. I have read that French women embrace natural hair colours rather than anything too extreme.

Clothing. What I have taken from the French woman is to wear what I like and what suits me, regardless of what's in fashion. I still try new things, but have come to get a better idea of whether it will suit me or not.

I also know now that I don't like floaty boho pieces, but feel altogether more polished in simple, fitting shapes in soft or bright colours paired with neutrals and not too much black. The process of thinning out my wardrobe is ongoing, distilling the pieces down into ones I love and wear and which look great on me.

Using my good things. I light expensive gift candles, eat off our good plates, and enjoy one of the few bottles of good wine we have stored away for a special occasion. My husband has said this to me more than once that he loves that I use my good things.

We have four gorgeous small glasses rimmed in 24 carat gold that have to be hand washed (I learned that after putting two in the dishwasher - it used to be a set of six). I never used them because... they had to be hand washed. A few months ago, I got them out of the cupboard, hand washed them and used them that night. It felt like such a treat! They really are beautiful glasses and I don't mind looking after them.

Same with some wine glasses which were a gift. When I broke one and had to replace it, one glass cost $30. It put me off using them for a while, but now I do again. I put these ones in the dishwasher. If they break, they break. Better to enjoy them than keep them for, what? The day that never comes?

My Nana died last year, and she was famous for keeping her good clothing in the wardrobe and wearing old clothing around the house. She bought beautiful, expensive clothing but didn't want to wear it (it was 'too good'). Now her daughters and grand-daughters are walking around in her lovely tops and scarves.

She also had boxes of scented body lotions and perfumes stored under her bed, with cheap supermarket body lotion in the bathroom. Perhaps that comes from growing up during the Depression. I'm just sad that she didn't get to enjoy it.

So now when I look into the bathroom cupboard after my shower in the morning, I use my most expensive body lotion first. It doesn't last forever you know. Even if all I'm doing is going to work or staying home. I don't have that many big nights out to save it for.

One such day last week when I had moisturised top-to-toe in rose-scented Crabtree & Evelyn my husband commented how nice I smelt when we hugged. And even if he's not there I enjoy it too.

Joie de vivre

Keeping my *joie de vivre* is much easier when I take notice of the small pleasures around me. Taking enjoyment in everyday life is the secret to happiness I think, more so than 'big' things. Well, both are good but I try to appreciate the little things as well.

Recently I was checking out our small freezer to see if there was anything for dinner that night (there was not) and I found a lone mini-croissant from not too long ago. Yay! I then had a yummy little bonus to have with my fresh fruit and raw nut breakfast. It was beautiful after being thawed and having five minutes in a hot oven.

I also feel grateful when the house is lovely and tidy and clean and I already have the washing hung outside, so I feel like I have the whole day stretching in front of me to do with as I please. Tomorrow I might be back at work but today, today is for (apart from a few household jobs) sewing, knitting, movie watching and general pottering.

Some days I find it hard to muster up any *joie de vivre* and know that I am not fun to be around, even I can't stand myself. I have a set of three tiny notebooks (with cute Montmartre and Parisienne line drawings on the covers) that my sister gave me and I am on to filling up the second one so far.

The notebooks are small enough to put in my shoulder-bag (which isn't very big) and they are filled with uplifting and inspiring quotes that I have collected over time. They might be a line from a movie, a phrase from a book, or a line from a blog or website. They also include little goals that I think of and health plans I have for myself.

I read through one of my notebooks until I come across something that will cajole me into a better mood or make me realise I am being a spoiled brat. Sometimes it happens within a split second which seems like a miracle. It really is true that our mind precedes all else. Napoleon Hill's Think and Grow Rich has the secret right there in the title.

I remember hearing on an audio CD that you can't just 'make dinner'. You have to think of what you're going to make and then go about checking that you have the ingredients and THEN make it. The same is true of us. We can't just be skinny or be stylish or be a better person. We have to think of it first and be in that frame of mind before the rest follows.

'Our life depends on the kind of thoughts we nurture. If our thoughts are peaceful, calm, meek, and kind, then that is what our life is like. If our attention is turned to the circumstances in which we live, we are drawn into a whirlpool of thoughts and can have neither peace nor tranquility.'
– Elder Thaddeus of Vitovnica

Reasons to smile

I found this list in English magazine 'Woman'. I liked all the tips so much I thought I couldn't not share them with you.

Often these types of lists are clichéd and pointless (if that's not too harsh). This one makes me want to smile more so I can be younger, happier, healthier and more popular.

Sometimes I forget to smile regularly. And a resting face often isn't just impassive, it's quite downcast. So I noted down this list to encourage me to smile more often. And like anything, the more often you do something, the more likely it is to become a habit, and your natural state.

People that smile a lot always seem more attractive to me, even if they're not model-good-looking. There really is not a face that cannot be improved with a smile. When I'm out walking in the mornings, I like to smile at other walkers I pass. Most smile back and may say 'good morning'. Some don't, but that's OK, hopefully smiles are catching. They really make you feel good.

Five great reasons to smile

1. Smiling makes us more attractive, so if you're trying to impress, a smile will draw people in.

2. A smile changes your mood for the better – even if you don't feel like smiling, it actually tricks the body into feeling better by releasing endorphins.

3. You'll look instantly younger. The muscles you use to smile lift the face, making you appear younger.

4. It lowers your blood pressure. When you smile there's a measurable reduction in your blood pressure readings.

5. Smiling relieves stress. It also helps to stop you looking tired, worn out and overwhelmed, so making you better able to cope.

Ways to bring more French chic into your life

When I'm feeling a bit workaday and hum drum, I like to remind myself of my original excitement for the French Chic lifestyle and make little notes to bring my thoughts back to that. These corrections from time to time keep me happy with my simple life and ensure I am on the track I want to be on.

Sometimes it's all too easy to get carried away with someone's glossy reports of that new and shiny doodad they've just bought. It's not me and I know it's not me, but it helps to have something that pulls me back – gently - to my core philosophy too.

It's really going back to basics, and I love that it reminds me of the early days of my enthusiasm about the world of French Chic.

Here are my ideas:

Eat as if in France – real, good food and perhaps look up the principles of the Mediterranean diet for ideas.

When I have a coffee or a cold **drink, don't eat at the same time** (French girls don't snack between meals). When I first started this, it was hard. I associated a morning cafe au lait with a muffin or something similar. Now I don't even think about eating anything, the coffee is enough mid-morning. I am now working on eliminating a snack at my after-work/pre-dinner drink time!

Enjoy yoghurt daily and a small piece of cheese every now and then.

Decorate like we live in a Parisian apartment – neat and tidy, streamlined and sparse, in a chic and stylish way of course.

Dress how I would imagine a French woman would – small, precise, quality wardrobe of limited colours which are best for me. A recognisable style which others can see easily is 'me'.

Keep hair regularly trimmed and coloured. Wash hair every second day and *do not* be tempted to stretch it out to a third.

Keep makeup light and fresh. Use the tiniest amount of foundation and spend time on my eye makeup.

Play French music at home, both old and new to keep that feeling of French charm and lightness within me.

How I act/my demeanour: To put a spring in my step, imagine my name is Dominique and I live in Paris. Pretend I am her as I go throughout my day.

Knit, crochet and sew – **be creative.** I read on annebarone.com a long time ago that having a handcraft to do prevented mindless snacking as you couldn't knit or do needlepoint if your hands were sticky from chocolate or greasy from potato chips. I always like to have my hands busy when I'm watching tv or a movie so try to keep a project by the sofa.

Read, both the chic-lit I enjoy plus books which challenge me a little. Also read more classics. My mother alternates writing styles – something fun and then something a bit more meaty so she has a good balance. In the past year or so I've read some thriller/crime mysteries and really enjoyed them.

Be light-hearted and channel Audrey Hepburn. She didn't take herself too seriously yet was a beautiful spirit.

Be slim and slender. Yes, spend time on our menus and creating good food, but don't make food a huge part of my life. Once I have sorted that day's and perhaps the next day's food, I can forget about it.

Watch a favourite movie or tv programme set in France. I have fond memories of the Peter Mayle tv mini-series A Year In Provence (based on the book) from the 90s and now have it on dvd. John Thaw and Lindsay Duncan star, and it has such a lovely warm feeling about it. Definitely comfort tv a la Francaise!

Living like a princess

So, I'm not a real Princess and I'm probably more the age of a Queen than a Princess, but I still like to dream of my Princess life. I like to think beautiful and elegant thoughts, and move like a Princess, the old-fashioned ones I used to read about when I was young girl. The kind that had long, bouncy hair and wore gowns with a bodice and full skirt.

I love the movie *Enchanted* even though it is sort of a children's movie. Amy Adams as the main character Giselle *is* rather enchanting as the movie title says and she gave me a renewed appreciation for the fairytale Princess stories of my childhood. Giselle dances around with a broom sweeping Patrick Dempsey's apartment, she has birds and mice singing and helping her and also whips up a dress for the ball, oops, from the living room curtains.

I don't do any of those things but I have found that dreaming of being Princess-like inspires me to remember my femininity and lightness, treat my darling like the handsome Prince that he is and flit around my home as if it is my castle. It really makes housework go much quicker and it becomes more pleasant. And the end result is a sparkling clean and fresh home fit for a Princess.

There used to be a website called the Princess Portal which I loved. I always felt uplifted and inspired to live a more beautiful life after reading one of this lovely lady's articles, however sadly it is no more. I saved a couple of things the author Skye wrote, including this:

The Princess Code

written by Princess Skye

A Princess inspires others to follow their hopes and dreams through pursuing her own.

A Princess greets everyone with a welcoming smile, melting the hearts of friends and disarming her enemies.

A Princess has dignity, which protects her from the opinions and spite of ignorant people.

A Princess always looks beautiful, even when she is asleep.

A Princess aims for perfection in every step.

A Princess should be given fresh flowers every day, even if she has to give them to herself.

A Princess grows in recognition and stature in proportion to how much she treats others as royalty.

A Princess reflects her inner beauty in her aesthetic choices.

A Princess goes to war against the violence of incivility with the weapons of etiquette and prodigal generosity.

A Princess lives each day from the heart, expressing herself freely and treasuring every moment.

A Princess has the right to spend her funds on beautiful things she does not need because beauty in itself is priceless.

A Princess should follow her heart and believe in her dreams, even if the whole world seems to be against her.

A Princess respects her environment and nurtures the beauty of nature.

A Princess is never too busy to give a kind word or smile where it is needed.

A Princess's most precious jewel is Hope, which lights her darkest days and shows her the beauty in every soul she meets.

--

When I am in a Princess mode I wear my most feminine and flattering clothing. Well, most of my clothing is flattering and those items that are not I am eliminating from my wardrobe, but not all are out-and-out feminine. Some can be stark or very simple, but I like to wear my few very feminine pieces when I am feeling in a Princessy way. It's nice to celebrate being born a girl!

One way to determine if clothing is feminine enough for your Princess days is to ask 'would a man wear this'. If the answer is yes and you still love the item, can you wear it in a feminine way? One example is jeans. Wear them with a pretty top and heels or ballet flats. Or if it's a t-shirt, choose a cut and/or colour that a man wouldn't be caught dead in.

Of course women can wear man-tailoring well but I still think you can be feminine. The cut of a woman's tweed jacket will be different to a man's. And you can zazz it up with feminine details such as makeup and jewellery.

Some take Princess style literally, but there are many ways you can add magical touches to your everyday life without looking like you're wearing a costume or acting in a play.

Be light and feminine in your movements.

Speak in a pleasant, musical voice.

Laugh a lot (in a pretty rather than a guffawing way).

Be easy to get along with. I love The Rules credo of '*being hard to get, but easy to live with*'.

Practice your mystique on every occasion, and have a small mysterious half-smile, in a friendly way of course.

Smile with your eyes as well as your mouth. In fact you can play up your eyes and play down your mouth when smiling, it's more effective.

All of this will filter through to the way you do other things in your life, because, as the saying goes *'the way you do one thing is the way you do everything'*.

I know I will have to put a disclaimer on this because some people may not like it. But that's okay. I know myself and know I am not a pushover. I know what I like and what I don't like and I create my life to my own recipe. Just because I have a fairytale Princess as one of my chic mentors doesn't mean I am not also a strong, independent and confident woman. *Vive la différence!*

A sensual life

At first glance, it may seem that a sensual life is the same as a sexy life. But it's not, it's far more than that. The base word of sensual is sense, and to live a sensual life is to live a life where you take full advantage of all five (or is it six?) senses.

I've certainly been guilty of relying too much on one sense in the past, the sense of taste. But we can make ourselves feel good without jeopardizing our svelteness by employing our other senses too. Let's go through the senses.

Sight. The sense of sight means you will notice beauty around you – particularly nature's beauty in the form of the sky, trees and plants, human being and animals. Man cannot build these things, so how did they get so perfect and well-designed? Who chose all the different and brilliant colours?

Even for non-religious or non-spiritual folk they must admit some form of higher power must have had a hand in somewhere.

There is also the beauty you can create yourself. Taking care of your home, your family and you, and creating a nurturing space in which to live. Dressing in the clothes that make you feel special and wonderful (and considering donating the so-so items, ones that have bad memories or taunt you for not fitting them) and taking the time to groom each day. I know that the times I don't shave my legs as often I'm not pushed for time, I'm just being lazy. And smooth, moisturised legs aren't just nice to look at, they feel nice to the …

Touch. Silky moisturised skin, clean and bouncy hair, clothes made from fabrics that feel good on your skin. I've donated a few tops that were quite nice on but they felt greebly again my skin. I think I made up that word but it describes the feeling, I just wanted to get the top off. One of my favourite things to do in the world is come home from work and change into one of my home outfits in softest cotton. It's pure bliss. Patting our cats, feeling the sun touch my face, a footrub from my love and having a good stretch all feel amazing and they are free. If you don't have someone to rub your feet, having a creamy lotion or a pot of body butter in the living room means you can give yourself a footrub whilst watching tv. Take the time to rub it in and really massage one foot at a time and if the product is very rich, have socks to put on afterwards so you can lie on the sofa without fear of getting it mucky. I promise your feet will feel like they are levitating off the sofa cushions with bliss.

Smell. I love pretty smelling things. I have a fairly decent (ahem) collection of fragrances and perfumed body lotions, creams and butters which I enjoy using every single day. I also like to spritz myself lightly when I get home from work and when I go to bed. What can I say, I love perfume.

Thankfully my husband is very laid-back and doesn't ask why I'm always wafting around on a pink scented cloud. There are also the wonderful aromas of fresh coffee whether it's being ground or brewed, bacon cooking (even though I've never eaten bacon and don't plan on starting), the honeysuckle growing on our fence, the lawns when they've just been mown, a freshly cleaned house, dinner roasting in the oven. There are so many wonderful scents around us if only we'd take the time to notice them. And maybe that's what sensual living is all about, being aware of our senses on a day to day basis and not rushing past all the micro-experiences that make up our life.

Sound. My most favourite and luxurious sound of all is silence and I love to indulge in it where possible. I also like to play a game with myself where I only speak when necessary because I know I talk quite a bit. I've realised I just don't need to go around narrating everything as I go! There are also other beautiful sounds in the form of music that you can create the soundtrack to your life with. I like to imagine I am in a movie when I am deciding which music to play. I have loads of cds on my iPod and I also love the internet radio stations such as Pandora where you can try out all sorts of genres.

Taste. We can't discount taste altogether though, just because I've decided I use this sense more than my others. It simply means I can be more selective and happy with smaller portions because I am savouring and enjoying the taste of what I'm eating rather than shovelling it in. One is chic, the other is not…

And the possible sixth sense, **intuitiveness.** I heard it explained really well the other day that your intuition is your subconscious which notices much more than your conscious. So having a hunch or intuition is actually your subconscious nudging you with information that you need, that your busy and distracted conscious mind has not picked up on. Isn't that cool?

Since I started thinking about the senses and that nurturing each one is the key to living a sensual life, I was excited to write them down and brainstorm ideas for each one so I could not neglect any one sense.

Chapter 7.
Real life inspiration

It's all very well to take your inspiration in through the written word, and it is one of my favourite ways simply because you can do it anywhere or anytime. However, nothing beats actually physically getting into a situation where you are inspired.

Something magical happens, and long after you can still remember the feeling you got. That is a very powerful force. Look for those opportunities where possible. They are around.

An evening with Mireille

When Mireille Guiliano visited my town promoting her book French Women Don't Get Facelifts, I was so excited. My mother emailed beforehand to let me know she was coming and I immediately booked my ticket.

It was a beautiful summer evening and the event 'Conversation with Mireille' was held at the Villa Maria vineyard in Auckland, New Zealand which looked absolutely stunning as I drove in.

Of course I put a lot of thought into what I was going to wear. My new Diane Von Furstenberg wrap dress looked to be a shoo-in but it was a very hot and humid day so I wondered if I would be too warm in its long-ish fitting sleeves. I decided on one of my other recent purchases, an army green Banana Republic coatdress and tan leather high-heeled sandals.

There were a lot of women already there when I arrived and many of them were milling outside. I saw inside the door that some women were already seated so I went in and bravely sat in the very first row, right in front of the lectern. I didn't want to miss a single breath.

She was fabulous. Mireille was very gentle and fun and seemed a genuinely lovely person. She read a few excerpts from the book and talked about the different categories, such as dressing, skincare, grooming, 'invisible' exercise and enjoying life.

I took good notice of her personal style too. Mireille wore a blouse in white and black with a *toile de jouy* type print and it seemed to be one of those uniquely French ones that are finely pleated/scrunched, the ruffled collar and placket edging certainly was. Her pants were classic and not tight at all, and she had mid-heel shoe-boots in embossed black suede.

You also couldn't help but notice Mireille's black epi-leather Louis Vuitton bag, centre-stage as it was. I'm not sure what the style is known as but I found some pictures of one called Bowling Montaigne which it may be.

And hanging slightly out of her bag was a scarf in a beautiful ochre colour. It was a pleated silky/acetate looking fabric and the shade was a good match for her hair (she must already know the trick that three personalised colours that are great for you are to match your hair, eye and skin colour).

Her makeup was subtle to the point of unnoticeable. Mireille talked about this during the evening. She said as she gets older she wears less, and said bright red lipstick is too much for her now, and that too much eye makeup emphasizes her wrinkles, so she wears very little. Of course there are women of a certain age who wear quite striking makeup and that is part of their 'look'. It all goes back to knowing yourself and being uniquely you. Apparently French women would be horrified to look like other women and want their own look that no-one else has.

I noticed Mireille's hands – she had short, neat nails, with either no polish or just clear. I always feel bad that I don't wear at least a pale pink polish, but the reality with my job is that it chips within one day, and even if you can't notice with a light colour, I know it's chipped and tacky. Opening shoebox after shoebox just shears that colour right off.

Mireille said there were usually two kinds of people who came to her book launches. Women who want to lose weight (particularly for her first book I suppose) and Francophiles. I tried to appear invisible at that comment because it is quite an embarrassing thing to be exposed as someone who is shallow enough to like something or someone just because they are French and stylish. But that's exactly why I was there, so I should own it.

She was surprised when her first book became a bestseller in France, because as she rightly said, why would a French woman listen to another French women living in America talking about being French. But the main reason French women liked her book was the nostalgia factor. They told her they remembered their mothers saying the same things to them that Mireille recounted.

About exercise Mireille said she and her French friends hated that word and did not use the gym. Of course some French women go to the gym but it is not as common as in other countries. One of her close American friends moved to Paris and ran gym classes there. When they caught up two years later, Mireille was stunned to find that her American friend did not speak one word of French. The reason was that all her clients were ex-pats and not French women! Mireille talked about walking being the best exercise, and said others also swam, cycled and did yoga.

I even got to speak directly to Mireille. At the end of her talk, audience members were asked if they had any questions. Not many people asked, and I had a sudden thought what an amazing opportunity this was but I couldn't think of anything to ask! I said to myself 'what is the best question to ask Mireille'. I then put my hand up and the presenter sitting with her handed me her microphone. I said to Mireille that she obviously travelled a lot (she was in London the previous week, she had mentioned earlier) and how did she pack, did she have the perfect capsule wardrobe and what were her travel secrets.

She told us that she never checked her bag but always had the small wheelie one that you could carry on. She said sometimes airports are so spread out you are walking for miles, and who wants to drag a big heavy bag around. She also said she had three items of clothing that she made four outfits from. I'm going to try and work that one out! She also said she always put tissue paper in between her clothing items.

That's another 'life of luxury' tip I thought afterwards. Tissue paper is not expensive (and often free – I save it up and never use it for anything) and you could reuse it over and over if you are careful. I am going to put some in my suitcase so I remember next time I travel.

After her talk we were told we could purchase her new book and have it signed if we wished. I was thrilled to have this chance and had put off buying the book hoping this would be the case. I have been reading it though as I already had it out of the library (so now I can return it!) and I love it.

I bought the book and joined the lengthy queue. When it came to my turn she was sweet and quite unassuming, very normal really! She wrote my name and signed hers. As I was about to leave and she was moving onto the next person I squeaked out at the last minute 'did she allow photos'. 'Of course', she replied. And she so thoughtfully moved a gift she was given off the seat next to her and pulled it up close for a better photo. She really is lovely and charming, and I'd be very surprised if it was an act. People can't fake that. As I was leaving I said to her 'I'll see you with your next book' to which she replied 'it will be about oysters… and carrots'.

I didn't take notes like I thought I might because I really wanted to be present and enjoy the talk, but I did jot down some when I got home of the things I remembered.

At one point she told the audience that if they don't change anything else in your life at all, add good yoghurt into your diet 'for one year', plain yoghurt that is made just from milk and culture. She reckons that one yoghurt a day will help you lose weight because 'without going into all of the science about it' yoghurt has fat-burning properties.

I'm not so much interested in weight loss these days but more focused on maximum nutrition, because I know if you focus on eating good, real nutritious food, your body and weight will be stable and happy. I had forgotten about yoghurt for a while though, so I bought some today to add to my fresh fruit and raw nuts for breakfast.

Mireille said of relationships that 'love' and 'laughter' are the two things to have. She said you can have one or the other and be quite happy, but to have both means you've really struck the jackpot.

To summarise, the message I took from Mireille in both her words and the way she comported herself, was to be relaxed and content, enjoy the fun side of life, and be gentle with and look after yourself in all ways.

As I drove home just after 8pm with the sun setting on a beautiful dark blue sky, I felt so grateful and fortunate to have been able to listen to and meet one of my favourite and most inspirational authors.

My trip to Paris

In 2001 I travelled to Paris. I spent a petite two nights/three days there on the way to London, but I'm so happy I have actually been to Paris. I travelled with a female friend who was running the London marathon. She had planned on going by herself and was talking about the trip.

Someone then said 'why don't you go too Fiona?' I was recently single after my first husband deserting me. I had just started a new job and was living in a new, much bigger city (by my choice, I didn't want to be single in the small-ish town I grew up in). I shared a house with my sister and two other flatmates.

I had the money, I just didn't know if I could get a month off work. Normally you have to work there for over a year to accrue three weeks, and I had only been there less than ten months. I'd never been to Europe though, and decided that if my boss would let me have the time off, I'd go.

He agreed! Somehow we worked out the extra days, maybe some were unpaid, or he carried them over to the next year.

Paris was our first stopover on the way to London, but funnily enough we flew into London and then onto Paris. From New Zealand it's a long trip. It was almost a full twenty-four hours later that we arrived at Charles de Gaulle airport in Paris.

My travel companion is much more gung-ho, can-do and gutsy than I am, so rather than pay for a taxi, we hopped onto the train. Amazingly we got to our hotel alright, near the Paris Opera. We stayed in a gorgeous French decor hotel (Millennium Opera), with a tiny lift that the metal cage doors rattled shut.

Our hotel was on Boulevard Haussmann and very central, which meant that Galaries Lafayette, the famed department store was a mere stroll down the road. My travel companion wore knit track-pants, a sweatshirt, running shoes and a bumbag. Oh dear. We weren't very close friends - my sister had rented a room in her house and that's how I knew her. In Paris I dressed up more than on any other stop on my trip.

On the first day I suggested we sightsee separately, saying to her that she would be bored with all the shopping I planned to do (she wasn't a very girly girl and shopping was low on her agenda). Even though I love nice things, I didn't plan to do much shopping at all, but I did plan to soak up the Paris atmosphere.

I wore a black knit just-below-the-knee skirt, a dark charcoal fine merino round neck long-sleeve top, maxi-net tights (like a large fishnet) or perhaps it was stockings, I don't remember. High heels, a grey faux-fur scarf, a camel-coloured leather shoulder bag and my blonde hair dried straight and pulled back into a low ponytail completed my Paris look.

I loved just strolling through the shops and up the back streets pretending I lived there and was out for an afternoon's shopping. My inner French girl Sabine was alive and well more than a decade ago, in fact I think I've always been a day-dreamer.

European men are different

On that same European trip I also spent a few days in Rome after Paris. Because of visiting these two cities, I dressed up. I packed a skirt and high heels even though I was travelling with a back pack.

My travel companion, on the other hand, wore sporty track pants (gathered at the ankles), a sweat shirt and a bum bag (fanny pack). Such a shame. One of our days was spent seeing the sights and the other, shopping, window shopping, and soaking up the atmosphere. On the shopping day I suggested we split up for that day and meet back at our hotel later on. I feel a little unkind about this, but I wanted to enjoy the ambience of Paris by myself, and in appropriate attire.

In Paris, one lunchtime when I was walking back to the hotel with my friend, a young man came up to me and asked if I would like to go out with him. 'I'm only in Paris tonight', I said. 'One night is all I need...' he replied. And not sleazy either! Rather, fun and flirty. I declined politely.

Next was Italy. The same travelling companion and I walking along a footpath in Rome, admiring beautiful building after beautiful building, wondering at what family-run trattoria we should dine that evening.

Next thing, a suave and svelte Italian gentleman on his scooter (of course, they were everywhere in Rome - young women in pencil skirts and high heels with open-face helmets on, balancing a coffee on the handlebars and stylish young men in fine cut suits) rides close to where we are walking, making kissy faces to us. Again, fun and flirty.

These light hearted encounters just add to your day. No wonder French and Italian women like to dress up!

True stories from Paris

My great-aunt has some amazing stories about her years of living and working overseas as a nurse. She was a private nurse for Elizabeth Arden's sister in the late 1960s in Paris. This lady was the behind-the-scenes person for the beauty company. My great-aunt would stay with her overnight in her Paris apartment and her household staff would be there during the day.

Miss Arden had to go to hospital for some reason, and couldn't decide whether to book into the American Hospital in Paris, or be privately nursed either at her home in Chantilly just outside of Paris, or in a suite at the Hotel Ritz. She finally decided not to stay at the Ritz as her dog didn't like the food there. Yes, really.

My great-aunt said in Paris you would see people sitting in the hotel restaurant, dog on a chair next to them, eating from their own plate at the table. Incredible.

My great-aunt also told me that when she worked at the American Hospital in Paris in 1969, she nursed Coco Chanel (the real deal). One evening Mademoiselle Chanel did not feel like having a bath or a shower, so had my great-aunt empty bottles of Chanel No. 5 into a basin for a sponge bath. When she was finished, my great-aunt was instructed to pour the fragrance down the sink.

During the same hospital stay, a very young Karl Lagerfeld came in to visit Mademoiselle Chanel. When I asked her if Coco spoke much, she said she never stopped talking, however it was in very fast French and my great-aunt was still learning to speak the language at that stage so didn't catch much at all. Such a shame! Imagine having a conversation with Coco Chanel and the questions you could ask her.

Chapter 8.
Inspiration from books and magazines

It's not often I get to finish a magazine or book without wanting to either tear a page out (magazine) or Post-it flag a page (book) to copy out a quote. I see inspiration everywhere I look.

True Pleasures

Below are two of my favourite quotes from True Pleasures: A Memoir of Women in Paris by Lucinda Holdforth.

'The Paris of my imagination is a site of pleasure and history and beauty. It's a place to recharge myself as a woman. Each time I come back here it's like greeting an older woman friend, one who is rather grand and imperious - a great dame, in fact - who likes me to look my best, to have my wittiest conversation to hand and to be on my toes all the time.'

And another,

'The house is small and modest, a sign of her commitment to financial freedom and independence.'

The house we rented before we bought our current home was rather small and modest, but rather than just exist in it and wait and wish for a bigger place, I decided to embrace its size, decluttering and making the most of things (it's not that we needed a bigger house, we just need less stuff).

We were very lucky in that it was thoroughly renovated immediately before we moved in, with everything whitewashed, brand new kitchen and brand new dark donkey-brown carpet. Every single light switch and light fitting was new, even hinges and handles on the doors (brushed silver). If we had to choose the decor, we would probably choose the one we ended up with.

Now that I am a homeowner, the sentiment still applies. Our home is medium in size and not that new. It still has the original kitchen and bathrooms. Rather than wishing for everything to be updated though, I am just happy to be paying off our mortgage quickly, and keeping our home neat and clean. I feel so grateful.

I love Lucinda's second quote as it reminds me we are being good stewards of our money by not wasting (whether rent or mortgage) our funds on a large abode. And if I find myself wishing for a bigger home, I remember the chic Parisiennes living stylish lives in their tiny apartments and all is well again.

How to seduce

Whenever I have a hair appointment I read a lot of magazines, because it always takes a while. I don't really buy magazines anymore, but I always enjoy catching up with them at the hairdresser's. At a recent visit an article in Grazia caught my eye – *'How to Seduce a Man'*.

Well, I had to take notes. All the suggestions were so good, I thought they would benefit me in day-to-day life and also, even though I am already married, with my husband. You see, they aren't all just about seduction, but how to be attractive generally. I really love articles like that.

I wrote down the headings, and now I'm going to remember, paraphrase and add my own notes.

Wear red. This colour makes you more attractive to men. I too often notice how nice a woman looks when they wear red. It makes your skin look a little flushed perhaps, in a good way. Whatever colour you wear (on your top half at least), picks up the colour on your face. That's why pinks and peaches are so flattering as well, and perhaps could be a less intense option for a top. And why black is not ideal, even though we all love wearing it – it picks up black circles under the eyes!

Show 40% of skin. I think this was aimed more at dressing up for an evening out. 40% is the ideal amount. Anything less and you risk sinking into dowdy territory, any more and you will end up seducing your man in a less chic way, and showing yourself off as being very available. It probably would work for daytime too. A French women is famous for showcasing just *one* part of herself, whether it's great legs, toned arms or a silky-smooth décolletage. If every single part is covered up you wouldn't really notice, but imagine a women in well-fitted jeans and slender-cut t-shirt, that when she turns around shows a back-revealing detail. Ooh la la.

Be well-rested. This article claimed that men were shown pictures of women from two groups – one group had plenty of sleep and one group had no sleep. Of course they chose the well-rested group as more attractive. I can't argue with that. And for heaven's sake don't wear a black top on a day when you didn't get enough sleep!

Smile thirty-five times an hour. Women who smiled every 1.7 minutes were considered more attractive than those who smiled less. Does that seem like a lot of smiling? I remember from my (second) wedding day I had sore cheeks the next day from smiling for photos and well-wishers. So perhaps a little less smiling than that. The charity shop near me has the most pinch-faced old bat behind the counter. Even when I am dropping off really nice donations she can't force a smile out. I bought a book from there a few days ago and she handed me my book and change and I actually waited until she made eye contact with me and then smiled at her and waited for the return smile... it eventually came, a tight, miser-ish little smile. Geesh, they don't cost anything love. I feel a bit mean about 'making' her smile, but it was fun. And on the other side of the scale, people I've met who I often think 'aren't they just so nice' are the ones that smile, a lot.

Touch him subtly. When you're talking to a man, whether it's someone you met in a bar, your boyfriend or your husband, make a point to subtly touch him to make a point. Perhaps on the arm or shoulder. Not too much though, don't be one of *those* women (an over-toucher Seinfeld would probably call her). I think non-bedroom touching is very important in a relationship. A quick shoulder-rub going past your man when he's sitting down, a touch on the hand, quick kiss on the neck.

Wear a spicy-floral fragrance. Apparently you will appear 5kg / 10 pounds thinner. And who doesn't want that? I was pleased to see that Chanel No. 5 has spicy components as well as powdery florals. There are many other spicy-florals that aren't as heavy as straight out oriental perfumes. Dolce Vita I know is one, from my days at Dior, as is the original Dior Addict in the dark blue bottle. One of my husband's friends used to give me a hug when he saw me and exclaim in raptures whenever I wore Dior Addict. After he met his wife, he did it a few times and then stopped. I think she had words with him that she'd rather he went into raptures over her instead. I don't blame her!

Be charitable and a better person. Even if they don't know it, men are always sizing up a potential female partner as the mother of his children. If he sees that you are a kind person he is likely to think more of you. I've read often that men want their women to be a better version of themselves. They put us up on a pedestal and look to us as the moral guider. That's a tall ask I know. It also makes me try and be a better person. Again, in my observations of other women, isn't it a not-nice shock to discover that someone you admired and thought to be lovely ended up being a bit sneaky or mean-spirited? I don't want to be one of those women. I want my husband to think I am saint-like, heavenly and kind-hearted.

Talk to him with head slightly tilted forward. Something about looking up at him and being slightly submissive. It sounds quite hard to do without looking silly. What I do know though, when you see aggressive women on tv (likely in a reality show like Top Model) they talk with their head held back and up, and look arrogant and aggressive. They don't exactly come across as feminine or even remotely likeable.

Wear a little makeup. Finally, the article says men may profess to like women *a la naturale*, with no makeup at all. The study shows another story though. The women with scrubbed clean faces were rated as less attractive as women who were very lightly made up. The key point was a contrast between features and skin. So mascara, lipstick, blush and defined brows are important. What I think it is that men don't like is makeup put on with a trowel and spider-leg eyelashes.

What would you add to this list? Care to refute anything? I would love to hear your comments. Wanting to be feminine and have men find you attractive is quite controversial in our modern Western society. But isn't that what French women have been doing forever? I know it's not for everyone, but for me, I love talking about all this girly stuff.

Supermarket Supermodel

I picked up 'Supermarket Supermodel' because the book title made me curious. It is written by Jim Cartwright, who also wrote 'Little Voice' (a play, and a movie).

It was a thoroughly engrossing and rather different book, and what impressed me most was that while the main character Linda was female, the author is male. He totally got inside her head. Linda is an English supermarket check-out operator, and after being 'discovered' becomes a famous supermodel.

One of the parts I really enjoyed reading was when Linda met Jackie Collins at a party. An odd situation, I know. I'm not sure if the author has met Jackie Collins in real life, but I just love his descriptions of her as an ultra-feminine, captivating and focused woman.

Here is an excerpt of the day after the party. Jackie has taken Linda home and gives her a bed for the night (she wasn't well at the party, and could not remember the address of the friend she was staying with). Linda wakes, hung-over, and has breakfast with Jackie.

Those few hours in her company gave me a world of wisdom, though there were no lectures or advice or anything like that. I can't describe it proper. It was just like she was an education in herself. She was all the education a young woman needed just by being alive.

The way she did things, taking a call, picking a flower, pouring a drink, sharing a joke with the maid, laughing, winking, watching the ocean. She was woman in all her fullness, a rose, beautiful, fragrant, feminine, but that didn't stop her from being powerful and who she wanted to be. It was like I was gathering it from her, getting the fragrance.

It was like the good fairy from the films when I was a kid, don't remember her giving much advice, it was just her presence made everything better, the touch of her magic got you on the right track and wicked witches and goblins disintegrated at her jewelled feet.

Suze had been a good teacher, she knew lots of things and could teach you stuff and tell you loads, but she wasn't what she taught, she wasn't it. Jackie was it. She really was everything Suze worked and strained to be, but Jackie was just it. It didn't really matter what she said or did but how she was.

We listened to the soul music and now and again she'd say let's change the track, and it was always right and took us one deeper or one higher or suited the next thing she was going to do. We both did the breath in at one point and smiled. Too soon it was time to go. She took care of everything, paid for my flight home and got her driver to take me to the airport.

Then I left LA and, resting in Jackie and the soul music, I flew home, flew home on it. I knew what I wanted now, I wanted to be like her. Strong, glamorous, independent, doing what she wanted but still loving and a woman.

from Supermarket Supermodel by Jim Cartwright

How to be happy

In the January 2011 issue of Real Simple the focus is on happiness. I hadn't even gotten into the body of the magazine before editor's page captured me. Let's face it, editor's letters aren't usually the best part of a magazine. They go through and point out highlights of that month's copy and I don't usually even glance at them.

This one though, struck a chord with me. Delving into how to be happy, the editor said happiness comes in small doses. When she was young she thought she would be happy when she was grown up and that happiness would coat everything 'like a blanket of snow, covering everything in sight with a dazzling, seamless beauty'.

Now that she is grown up, she knows that isn't the truth, and that happiness is more than likely to be found in the little things. Things such as:

- Changing from high heels to slippers when she arrives home.

- Eating a piece of chocolate.

- Watching a funny tv show.

- Reading a short story.

- Hugging.

- Wiping the crumbs from the kitchen counter.

I agree with all of these, and it's true, they do make you feel happier. In any one day, these things are guaranteed to lift my mood and make me feel happier:

- Clear the dining table of 'stuff'. Put it all back where it belongs.

- Ditto the living room. Straighten it up.

- Enjoying a cool glass of water.

- Re-watching a favourite television programme or movie.

- Reading or re-reading a fun and enjoyable chick lit book.

- Going for a walk.

- Enjoying the house after I have vacuumed and dusted.

- Hanging laundry on the line and then bringing it in to fold after a sunny day.

- Using up the last of something – body lotion then recycling the bottle or vegetables in the fridge for a slowcooker meal or soup.

- Putting a casserole on in the Le Creuset and then enjoying the aroma as it cooks

- Decluttering and organising a drawer or cupboard.

- Washing the dishes by hand.

- Finishing off one job before starting another, rather than multi-tasking.

- Presenting a meal to my man and hearing happy noises from him about it.

- Changing the bathroom hand towel frequently so it is always clean and dry.

With the world being such a place of turmoil, both man-made and with natural disasters, it is sometimes easy to feel scared or fearful for the future. I think it's very important to keep our homes as our sanctuary of peace and order. An oasis to come back to.

And by giving out an energy of positivity and calm, we not only keep ourselves healthy and happy, but it affects others around us in a good way too.

We do what we can for those close to us who are in need of help, or by donating to charities, but it's not going to do anyone any good if we fall to bits. By taking small bites of happiness where we can, will go a long way to helping us enjoy this precious, short life that we have.

The Paris Winter

I have just finished reading The Paris Winter by Imogen Robertson. This book is not my usual, in that I am not that fussed with historical fiction and generally do my best to avoid it. I much prefer stories set in modern time. But Paris swayed me and so I found myself visiting (and much enjoying) 1909.

The tv series Mr Selfridge has just started here and we've seen the first two episodes, so I was tickled to see that this is also set in 1909. I loved the fact that I had a pictorial view of what the times were like in that era and could imagine its Paris equivalent, just across the water from London.

This book is a slower read than my normal choices, in that it took me about a month to read when usually I can get through a title in two weeks, sometimes even one week if it's a ripper. The last one-weeker I had was Sophie Kinsella's latest recently.

The Paris Winter is like a hearty and delicious French meal in that you want to chew it slowly in order to fully appreciate the flavours. I actually found myself reading more carefully to ensure I took in the descriptions and words used. The author has quite a magical quality to her writing that makes you remember all the characters and never be confused about what is happening.

The pace carries you along too as I never felt like I was pushing myself to read it. Life is too short for that I have decided, and if I find myself making excuses about picking up a book I have started, I just flag it and move on.

I chanced upon this title from reading a brief but favourable review in a magazine. I am glad I did not know too much of the storyline before I started, so I could enjoy its unfolding set during what was quite a major part of French history. You will probably want to Wikipedia this event as I did afterwards.

A wonderful part of The Paris Winter was a handful of pages at the end of the book outlining who were characters that were taken straight from history, and details of others who were based on or inspired by real people.

It also has an art component, in that the main character is a young English woman who has travelled to Paris to attend art school. There are fabulous descriptions of art peppered throughout the book that even I as a non-artist can appreciate, and it all ties in beautifully at the finish.

One fun thing I enjoyed doing during reading was to Google Map some of the street names that featured in this book, such as Rue de Seine and Place Pigalle in Paris. Using Street View I could have a look around and imagine the characters living there and walking down the footpaths.

I love Google Maps so much and often pop into New York City or Paris for a fix. I even visited Moscow the other evening. Such fun! I really am a cheap date. Sometimes I visit the main parts and other times I drag the little yellow man onto a random suburban street to see how ordinary people in that area live and what their houses look like.

I copied down a few quotes from The Paris Winter as I read it. You might enjoy them too.

(Character Tanya, a well-to-do young Russian woman, also studying art at the same art school):

'Always have the means to a graceful exit to hand – don't you think that is one of the best lessons we learn? I always have a gold sovereign sewn into my travelling dress. Actually half a dozen, so the line isn't spoiled.'

(Main character Maud, in an upmarket jewellery store in Paris):

There were three other women in the shop, all moving with the slow graciousness of wealth. They were as magnificent and polished as the shop itself.

Chapter 9.
Inspiration from movies and television

I'm not one of those people that says 'oh I never watch television' and make you feel bad about yourself because you do. I love television and watch a programme or movie most nights.

I need something to be doing with my hands though (or else I'd eat), so I either file my nails or knit. That way I can enjoy television guilt-free (all those non-television people must be getting to me. Just kidding).

Downton Abbey

I've taken a long time to investigate the world of Downton Abbey. I'd been ignoring it for a while but couldn't miss someone raving about it at seemingly every corner. Even though I usually avoid period dramas like the plague, I knew I would have to watch Downton Abbey to see what all the fuss was about.

It was amazing. Such a well-written drama, witty dialogue and laugh out loud funny moments (mostly over Dame Maggie Smith's lines which were delivered in her inimitable way). Julian Fellowes, the writer, is a very clever man.

It's hard to choose a character, but if I could most choose one to be like, it would be Lady Mary Crawley. I adore the way she speaks, in a low, slow voice and it's rare to see her flustered or over-excited. She is very calm and measured. All the women are elegant and gracious and inspire me to be more lady-like.

Amongst the backdrop of their very privileged (and endangered) lifestyle, I love that the women in the family cultivate simple pleasures such as needlepoint, reading and taking tea. Everyone speaks quite formally to one another, and if there is a cross word, it is either said straight, or in some cases couched in very witty and clever phrase.

The women dress very modestly but still fashionably. As the series progress, seeing the twenties fashions were a real treat and I'd happily wear those today. The women in the family always have their hair either in a chic updo, or styled into a faux bob. You realise just how long their hair is when they are dressing for bed at night time, but it is never down and loose in public (and by public I mean the rooms of the house where the men are, as well as outside the house).

Both men and women dress very formally and take the time to make themselves look attractive. It's not all about comfort – no-one slouches around in track pants and ugg boots there. I'm not saying I want to go back to corsets, but we have gone quite far the other way which is a shame.

Their huge castle must be freezing, and the way they dress in this environment is quite impractical, but that's the wonderful thing about Downton Abbey, 'practical' doesn't ever seem to be in their vocabulary. They dress up in beautiful clothing, change for dinner every night and have a valet or a ladies maid to help them dress. You don't have to do your own laundry and every little thing is done by someone else. All you have to do is enjoy your life (until the money runs out of course). Apart from the finance thing, doesn't that sound glorious?

I believe watching this programme has had a positive effect on me. Having it as a mind influencer makes me feel more ladylike myself, more feminine and gracious. I do not want to swear or raise my voice. I am content to be serene and feminine and fill my life with good jobs and a life well lived.

How to be a lady

A television series I loved and got a lot out of was *The Ladies of Hedsor Hall*. A group of rowdy young American women were sent to Hedsor Hall Finishing School in England. Aside from the inevitable cat fights, I really enjoyed the programme.

I would have dreamed of attending something like that myself, although these girls could have eaten me alive. And it's only now that I'm older that I can appreciate the lessons.

Hedsor Hall has a crest which stands for everything that defines a true lady - 'dignity, discipline and grace'.

The girls had a few rules when they first moved in:

- No swearing

- No excess drinking

- Lights out at 10pm

- Act like ladies at all times

They sound like not unreasonable rules to live life by in general.

Each girl was given a set of pearls to wear while they attended finishing school. The headmistress told them 'pearls become brighter and shinier with wear over time. Wear them to remind yourself you are a lady'.

Tidying up their appearance, the teachers asked them to aim for 'neat and tidy' and wear their hair off their face, with hair styled 'like a lady, not a 12 year old girl'. A smooth ponytail is ladylike for example, whereas pigtails are not.

They were given classes in various areas and I had to take notes. It's never too late to refine oneself, I feel.

Deportment. Sit up straight. The girls were taught to walk with a book on their head, and even tried walking with a book *and* a glass of water on their head. The book-walking was more successful and looked more natural than the book-and glass-walking.

Falconry, pheasant shooting. Just the usual everyday pursuits you might follow in the English countryside.

Art class, flower arranging. They actually created really pretty and professional looking flower arrangements (in oasis on a dish, rather than in a vase).

Fine wines. Some of the girls refused to spit the wine out, not wanting to waste it. I'm afraid I might be like that, but if I was in esteemed company I'd hope I would follow the lead of the others.

Social etiquette. Making conversation is about making people feel comfortable. It is bad manners to interrupt someone when they are speaking. A lady drinks on certain occasions and not to excess.

Anger management. Learning how to be a lady is learning how to manage your anger and control your emotions. Find an outlet for your anger (in their case they went fencing. As you do).

Dancing. In the elegant world of a lady, mastering dances such as the waltz can demonstrate grace and refinement.

Table etiquette. To honour your host, try any food that is put in front of you. Try to finish 2/3. Of course they chose the foods which would challenge the girls most - haggis, lamb testicles are the few I remember. I doubt I would ever come across a dinner party where delights such as these are served, but I would give it a good go and not complain and retch. I don't eat pork products but have had a couple of occasions where I have because I am somewhere as a guest. Of course if you are vegetarian or vegan for ethical reasons it is different, but if, like me, you don't eat something just because you don't care for it, it can't hurt to be polite to your host or hostess.

Sexual etiquette. Men are hunters. Men love the chase. You have to be that prize. The prize that that person will want to come home to. Naturally their former behaviour of hooking up with guys they'd met in a bar that night was frowned upon.

Appearance makeovers. Hair is taken back close to the natural colour and is styled to be 'neat and prim'. All facial piercings are removed and makeup is applied in neutral colours. 'Looks aren't everything but they are important. First impressions are made as soon as you walk into a room'.

The Disciplinarian (one of the teachers had this title - isn't it wonderful?) said of her class: 'The trouble with these girls is that they all live in their little boxes, filled with alcohol, men and a complete lack of ambition. In order to be really successful in life, you've got to experience new things... expand your horizons'.

I feel lucky that I had rather a better influence in life than a lot of these girls. There were some very sad stories. I have never felt the need to start a bar brawl, or to have my eyebrow pierced (at the tamer end of the scale). I have my mum to thank for trying her best to mold me into a lady from a young age.

Some of her words I can still recall: 'Speak properly', 'at least try something once before you say you don't like it', 'horses sweat, men perspire, ladies glow' and 'airports have lounges, Fiona, homes have living rooms'. My sister and I were taken complainingly to the theatre. But thankfully some of her lessons have rubbed off on me.

So won't we all put our pearls on today and head out into the world to 'be a lady'?

A perfect afternoon on the sofa

One of my favourite feel-good movies is '*A View From The Top*' starring Gwyneth Paltrow. It's just so silly and funny, but at the same time really motivational, *and* it includes scenes of Paris. Not to mention Gwyneth's character is made over during the movie from tacky to chic. Le sigh. No wonder I adore this movie.

I love this quote from Candice Bergen's character, said with a twangy Texan accent:

'*No matter where you're from, no matter who people think you are, you can be whatever you want, but you gotta start right now. Right this second in fact*'.

Candice is Gwyneth's mentor in the movie, a former flight attendant who has retired and written a book on success.

Watching the movie I was thinking to myself, I would really like to read that book. Shame it doesn't exist in the real world.

After watching the movie I am motivated to do better in all aspects of my life - at work, in my slimming efforts, being a good person. The list goes on. I love it when movies do that.

Chapter 10.
Reader Questions

I love receiving questions from readers. I'm always happy to give a different point of view, and they often make me think about things differently or give me exciting inspirational thoughts.

Keep them coming, lovely blog readers!

Reader Question #1

Wendy from Canada wrote and asked me –

"How do you regain your chicness when you have "fallen off the wagon"? For example, last Fall I bought some new clothes, improved my hair and makeup, lost a few pounds and had been doing a lot of interesting reading about the chic lifestyle. I felt really good!

Now I am feeling blah- don't feel chic at all. Just received some recent photos of myself from a family dinner where I look terrible (of course my sister circulated them widely.)

Does this happen to you? How do you get the chic feeling back?

How do the French gals keep feeling chic consistently? Constantly buying new things and treatments is not an option for me.

Dear Wendy,

I think this question is such a great one. I know exactly what you mean about things being blah. I highly doubt French girls buy new things and have treatments to feel better. They don't throw away their money like we (I) do (used to).

In your family photos do you mean you look unchic because you have gained weight and your clothes don't look as good as you imagined? I usually find this is the main thing - I have been slack with my chic eating and kilos sneak on. Well they don't sneak on, but I ignore them for a while. Or sometimes the way I've done my hair is not flattering (usually from doing the least I can get away with - terrible!).

Just as you have listed what you did last year - buying some new clothes, improving hair and makeup, watching what you eat and becoming a bit slimmer in the process and keeping up with your reading, I think you may have answered your own question. You probably won't need to spend any money though - you already have the new clothes, it's just a matter of fitting better into them.

I think for me I get all enthused at a change and after a while it becomes routine, but rather than let it stay as my new 'French-inspired regime' I slip back to old habits. We have to remind ourselves constantly, and re-remember what it was that inspired us - go back to the books or websites you read.

Anne Barone is where my initial excitement for the French life came from and I still get a thrill picking up one of her books. It brings back to me that magical feeling that I had from discovering something new and fun.

Printouts I have kept, magazine articles I have torn out and books I have in my home library all remind me and re-excite me too. Can you remember where it was first that you heard about chic French women, the European way of life, being chic and slim? Try going back there.

And of course, maybe you are just tired out and a bit overwhelmed if you have a lot on your plate. It's amazing how fast good intentions of chic changes fly out the window when life happens. In that case it's a matter of dealing with what you have to and making the most of what little energy you have left. Keeping up with the basics of self-care is a good goal during busy times.

Making lists of how I want to be is a great inspirer too. I make lists of the attributes that my most elegant self possesses, my ideal Paris girl wardrobe, how my dream home looks and functions, just to name a few. Reading through them helps me want to be that way and resist temptation or make the extra effort. At the very least I can daydream.

Think of yourself as a project and advise yourself accordingly as if you were a wise, older (probably French) girlfriend. What would you say? It is so easy to give others advice, and it is quite effective to view yourself from without. I always come up with really good ideas for myself (whether I take them on is another matter altogether).

Even at the end of the day it's not too late to start afresh. If your day has been frazzled and stressful, why not choose an early night over opening a kingsize bar of chocolate and reality tv. How much more nicer (and infinitely more chic) would it be to wash your face and then read in your tidied-up bedroom with soft music playing.

And then, there is always the option of being realistic. It's quite a relief to think 'I don't have to be anyone other than who I am. I can make the most of what I have and be happy with that.' After all, what is more attractive than a big smile and healthy self-confidence about a person. Sometimes when

I'm sure people are looking at me thinking 'who does she think she is' (and I am feeling suitably intimidated), how are we to know they are not thinking the exact same thing?

Reader Question #2

Dear Fiona,

There is magic in everything you write. It is more than just sharing how you choose to live your life. I noticed that every time after reading your post I feel emotionally uplifted/lighter, calmer, happier and more optimistic... I would like to learn how to maintain an authentic positive vibration.

There is something that makes me very sad sometimes. It is relationship dynamic with my parents. They were too busy living their own lives when I was growing up with grandparents. Now when I am almost 37 they need more space in my life than I am available to offer. It takes me to very dark place emotionally and has a negative effect on my productivity.

How to start over and be happy regardless of what past was like? How to protect yourself emotionally from relatives that make you sad? How to build healthy boundaries while still remaining polite?

Thank you.

Dear Anonymous,

Since you left this comment I have been thinking about what kind of answer I could write. I feel reluctant to actually advise someone as it seems such a big responsibility. I will give it a try though.

My main thought is to tell the truth. Tell your parents how you feel, how they make you feel, and that you want to change the way things are in the future.

If you don't feel brave enough to start this conversation face to face, do it in an email or a letter. That way you can edit what you want to say before you 'say' it, and they can get a chance to digest it. Hopefully then it will lead onto a worthwhile conversation.

I sent my Dad an email a few years ago about something that was bothering me. I felt sick when I had sent it, but we had a good conversation afterwards and I felt infinitely better.

Anything big to talk about is always going to be hard, but worth it. It will feel like a weight has been lifted from you.

If you worry about what to say to them, just say the truth. Say you have been feeling sad about them and feel pulled between them and your life. Let them know they weren't there for you then and that you have made your own life without them because of this.

See where that leads. If they aren't willing to change, then there's not much else you can do, but at least you tried to fix the problem. Hopefully they will be willing to meet you half way (or better still, more than half way) and this could be a brilliant new phase of life, for all of you.

Remember, we only have one life as us, why let it tick away with regrets and unhappiness. If there is something bothering us about our life, it is in our best interest to try and fix it.

To address your other question about maintaining an authentically positive disposition. I try to keep my energy level positive by not dwelling on unpleasant or sad things.

Because I am very sensitive, as I can probably imagine you are, these sorts of things really get me down. It could be a tragic newspaper article, a sad situation about someone I know, or good people struggling to make ends meet. I still live in the real world, but if there is something I have no control over, I try not to think about it.

I read books that make me happy: spiritually uplifting ones, chick lit, my French Chic library and many more.

Our mind is like a garden some say – if we don't plant flowers (good thoughts), then the weeds will take over (negative thoughts). If a weed pops up, replace it with a flower to crowd out that weed. As time goes on the flowers will regenerate naturally, as positive thinking is just as much a habit as negative thinking.

Make time for things you do that make you happy. A few examples of my own:

- Yoga classes

- Walking outside

- Carrying out my household chores with plenty of time to spare so I am not rushed and can enjoy doing them

- Going to see a movie by myself

- Reading at any time of the day

- A home spa day or evening

- Pottering

- Quiet time to myself

- Sewing, knitting, needlework, patchwork, crochet

- Window shopping and seeing what is new out there without spending a cent, except perhaps for a cold drink or a coffee

- Early nights

- Planning ahead and being organised

- A tidy, clean, orderly, peaceful home

- Having a pet

Think about your own list and do these things more.

Chapter 11.
Inspiring words

I am in awe over the power of words. Whether written or spoken they can evoke such intense emotion, ignite or calm us. How is that? However they work, I am so grateful for their existence.

'Manners are a sensitive awareness of the feelings of others. If you have that awareness, you have good manners'. - Emily Post

I have an A4-size spiral bound hardcover notebook that sits on my bookshelf among my books. A pen hangs in its spiral binding, ready for a quote inscription. When I'm reading a book and want to remember a passage I write it in this notebook. It can be a piece of poetry (even though poetry's not my favourite thing, sometimes the bits are good). I write the date too which is quite helpful and interesting.

'I have never had anything to do with the kind of fashion that is influenced by the press or identified with the spirit of the season. My clients come for me, they come back each season for my spirit'. - Giorgio Armani

Every once in a while I have a flick through this notebook and are newly re-inspired. The kind of quotes which might be lost if noted down on a piece of paper because they are so small, these are the quotes this book houses. And reading through them they give me a sense of what is me.

'What if you gave someone a gift, and they neglected to thank you for it - would you be likely to give them another? Life is the same way. In order to attract more of the blessings that life has to offer, you must truly appreciate what you already have'. - Ralph Marston

I'm sure to others they would mean almost nothing, but that's the beauty of the personal notebook. You don't have to explain why you enjoy a certain collection of words.

'It is true that some manifestations of the slow philosophy do not fit every budget. But most do. Spending more time with friends and family costs nothing. Nor does cooking, walking, meditating, making love, reading or eating dinner at the table instead of in front of the television. Simply resisting the urge to hurry is free'. - 'Slow' by Carl Honore

What I like most about gathering passages that speak to me all in one place, is that even though they can seem quite disparate, reading through them at a later date I can see the common thread that links them all.

I just love life. I love people. I love to write, that's my gift. I love to sing. I have a good attitude. I like to think I shine from the inside. - Dolly Parton

(I think Dolly's wonderful. She's an amazing singer/songwriter, a gorgeous person and seems to have been around forever.)

If we believe in magic, we'll live a magical life. – Anthony Robbins

(I just love this saying, it's one of my favourites and always makes me feel so good when I come across it again.)

Happiness is a daily decision. – Unknown

Once you replace negative thoughts with positive ones, you'll start having positive results. – Willie Nelson

(I love Willie too. His music is so calming and catchy and he seems really laid-back. My dad is a big fan also, and he heard Willie being interviewed once. Willie said his secret to good health and longevity was a big lungful of fresh air out his open bedroom window each morning. My dad said of that 'I don't think it's the fresh air he's breathing in'.)

From a television programme on driving safely in icy and snowy conditions:

The key is not to look at obstacles ahead, but instead to the route ahead. The human brain is hard-wired to look at the problem, but we must look away from the problem.

(I relate this to negativity. We are hard-wired to look at the negative side of things but we would do better to focus on the positive, if it's the direction we wish to go in.)

A positive attitude brings strength, energy and initiative. To think negatively is like taking a weakening drug. – Unknown

A person who has good thoughts cannot ever be ugly. You can have a wonky nose and a crooked mouth and a double chin and stick-out teeth, but if you have good thoughts they will shine out of your face like sunbeams and you will always look lovely. - Roald Dahl

To remain confident and positive, think about your goals all the time. – Brian Tracy

(I have many Brian Tracy quotes noted down all over the place. I can really relate to the things he says.)

You will never change your life until you change something you do daily. The secret of your success is found in your daily routine. – John Maxwell

Remember that the sudden decision to stop fighting, and just go with the flow, can be incredibly releasing. Resistance is just so draining. There is

a beauty to gracious acceptance, an energy that leads to peace. – Nikki Gemmell in Pleasure: An Almanac for the Heart

(I don't take this to mean fighting literally, but in any way you are resisting something. Change perhaps?)

Cheerfulness and content are great beautifiers, and are famous preservers of youthful looks. – Charles Dickens

And one more, because it's just so cute:

I know that dogs are pack animals, but it is difficult to imagine a pack of poodles… And if there was such a things as a pack of poodles, where would they rove to – Bloomingdales? – Yvonne Clifford

Desiderata

No matter how many times I read the Desiderata I never tire of it. It has such relevance, even today (*especially* today - our modern world would do well to just. slow. down).

Its words have such power. They slow my heart-rate in a relaxing way and all my muscles un-tense. My brain changes into a lower gear and my mindset shifts.

Go placidly amid the noise and haste,
and remember what peace there may be in silence.
As far as possible without surrender
be on good terms with all persons.
Speak your truth quietly and clearly;
and listen to others,
even the dull and the ignorant;
they too have their story.

Avoid loud and aggressive persons,
they are vexations to the spirit.

*If you compare yourself with others,
you may become vain and bitter;
for always there will be greater and lesser persons than yourself.
Enjoy your achievements as well as your plans.*

*Keep interested in your own career, however humble;
it is a real possession in the changing fortunes of time.
Exercise caution in your business affairs;
for the world is full of trickery.
But let this not blind you to what virtue there is;
many persons strive for high ideals;
and everywhere life is full of heroism.*

*Be yourself.
Especially, do not feign affection.
Neither be cynical about love;
for in the face of all aridity and disenchantment
it is as perennial as the grass.*

*Take kindly the counsel of the years,
gracefully surrendering the things of youth.
Nurture strength of spirit to shield you in sudden misfortune.
But do not distress yourself with dark imaginings.
Many fears are born of fatigue and loneliness.
Beyond a wholesome discipline,
be gentle with yourself.*

*You are a child of the universe,
no less than the trees and the stars;
you have a right to be here.
And whether or not it is clear to you,
no doubt the universe is unfolding as it should.*

*Therefore be at peace with God,
whatever you conceive Him to be,
and whatever your labours and aspirations,
in the noisy confusion of life keep peace with your soul.*

*With all its sham, drudgery, and broken dreams,
it is still a beautiful world.
Be cheerful.
Strive to be happy.*

Lovely. A daily read I think, would be medicine for one's head.

How to Be Slim and Healthy:
A French-inspired journey to slimness and good health

Chapter 12.
Being slim

Over the years I've spent time wondering why eating and weight is such a big deal for me. It shouldn't be, but it is and I know it's the same for many women around the world. I've often sighed to myself 'if only I'd been brought up in France, I wouldn't always be trying to figure out this diet thing because I would have grown up with a much healthier view on eating'.

Whether that's true or not I don't know, but I do know that many French (and other European) people I've met over the years have a very different take on eating and are for the most part slim and healthy.

Even though I grew up in a loving family where my mother cooked healthy and balanced meals at home each night, I've come to realise that I have taken a few food habits from childhood through to adulthood, the main one being the 'treat' habit. This treat habit means that my default thinking is 'what can I get away with eating' and 'what would taste yummiest', rather than 'what would be healthy and nourishing' which seems really boring to me.

When I'm craving potato chips and ice cream, I somehow imagine if I was born French, I'd naturally choose the healthy option and be happy with it.

But I know that habits can be changed, as can your thoughts. It's the untangling of those long-held beliefs that keep me tethered to foods that do not serve me that is the ongoing project. The project of retraining my mind to become one of a naturally slim person.

Avoiding overeating

One night when my husband went out to a fund-raising quiz night with a group of his friends, I had the house and evening to myself and it was all about me, me, me. In the past I have looked forward to such an evening as a 'treat night' where I would think about what I wanted to make myself for dinner and also plan what crap I was going to eat as well.

I would cruise the aisles of the supermarket shopping in preparation for the evening. There would be hard jubes, popcorn, chocolate and ice-cream (any or all of). So foul I know, and I would feel disgusting afterwards. Just how is this a treat Fifi? As I was thinking of going out food shopping, I thought about the French Chic life.

I pictured myself reading my French Chic inspiration and being chic and slender ideal-French-girl Sabine rather than a piglet on a sofa with junk food. Just imagining this was all it took to change my mindset from 'treat night' to 'French Chic night'.

All I bought at the supermarket was a piece of salmon and some milk.

I made myself the Jo Dinner as I call it. My mum Jo eats salmon and stir-fried vegetables five nights a week, she would probably have it seven if she didn't spend two nights staying overnight at her job in a private girls school. People often compliment her on her complexion. I think it's all that salmon like Mr Perricone says, along with a consistent skincare regime of course.

My stir-fry vegetables last night were carrot, broccoli, cauliflower, onion, garlic, capsicum, celery, mushrooms and green beans, in lemon infused olive oil since I was having fish. I've run into trouble before when making stir-fry for the two of us when all the different vegetables add up and I end up with a wok overflowing with goodness. It's not really the best start to the meal when your husband says 'this is getting ridiculous' in a good-humoured way (and he's a big eater).

Is it possible to binge on vegetables I wonder? After a stir-fry I always have a ready-made lunch for the next day. Last night was no exception, I still made twice what I needed even though I only used half of a carrot, a few florets of broccoli, three or four beans, three mushrooms etc. Those veges really play up in a wok and *expand*.

In the background while I was cooking played the latest Buddha Bar XII cd – it is so me – the inner leaflet has French imagery *including* the Eiffel Tower, and CD 1 in the set is called La Vie En Rose. I almost swooned when I realised all this. It's not dissimilar to the other Buddha Bar cds but I like that. It's new, but familiar.

Before dinner I had a glass of Chardonnay with Laughing Cow cheese which I'd wanted to try for a while. It is extremely delicious spread on crackers.

Later on I watched an episode of the television series The Starter Wife. One of the characters attends AA and she reminded a character leaving rehab about 'one day at a time'. I thought to myself that would be a good credo for anything you wanted to achieve in life, whether it is overspending, overeating, or even living the French Chic life.

It's hard to imagine you doing (or not doing) something for the rest of your life and that scares you into going back to how you were before. If I say I can never have a mini-pigout again, I would likely fixate on that. By saying 'just get through this day' eating healthfully and in reasonable proportions, well, this is much more achievable.

Countdown to 40

A few months before I turned forty, I realised that my weight was still a bother to me. Rather than get all worked up about it though, I relaxed and thought to myself, how can I change this?

Still no to Weight Watchers, it's too strict for me, but giving myself free rein is a recipe for disaster. I sat down and drew up some guidelines for the way I want to live, to enable me to slim down slowly and quietly.

My guidelines are not a diet, and there are no quantities listed. Here they are (I called them Countdown to 40, just for fun) −

Sunday to Thursday − alcohol-free nights
Friday night − Bubbly Friday (we've had Bubbly Friday for years)
Saturday night − snacks and drinks

This means I've cut down drinks to two nights a week (from probably 5-7 nights, even one glass of wine each evening adds up to a lot of calories) and I only eat snacks one night a week. I've decided I would rather have some camembert and crackers than potato chips, but if I want potato chips that's fine too, but only on Saturdays.

Salad with lunch every day
Vegetables with dinner every night

Protein at every meal, eg:
- Egg with breakfast
- Tuna with lunch
- Lean meat or fresh fish with dinner

One piece of fresh fruit every day

If I crave something sweet after a meal – 1-2 squares dark chocolate
If I crave savoury snacks, a small amount of rice crackers and cheese

Early nights – in bed by 9.30pm at the latest, preferably 9pm, to give plenty of boudoir time for reading and moisturising before lights out at 10pm.

Green tea first thing in the morning with blog time (6am)
Drink water all day

Two yoga classes per week
Three one hour walks per week (two included to and from yoga)

I have to say, having my guidelines has really helped me stay on track and have a balanced week with plenty of nutrition and good sleep. I started out by writing down what my perfect week would look like and added things as I thought of them.

I also like that they are not just about food, but incorporate lifestyle habits to aim for as well. I am still using my Chic Eating principles most of the time too (I can have anything I like as long as it is 'Chic' and 'Real').

If I ever feel like slacking off, maybe pouring a glass of wine on a Wednesday, I remember my Countdown to 40 list and I feel newly remotivated. I also have the Word document open on my laptop most of the time, so I see it whenever I'm on the computer.

Becoming and staying slim

I've always had a love/hate relationship with dieting. I love the thought of a clean start with a new eating plan and exciting goals, but I'm also worried about jinxing myself. It seems that I can stick it out for so long before falling off the healthy living wagon.

For the way my mind is, I find it doesn't work for me to have a goal time such as a birthday, Christmas, wedding or summer. I just rebel against it straight away.

The trouble with me is that I am not a naturally thin person, who happily chooses the low-calorie option. My sister at one stage had an obsession with carrots and couldn't get enough of them. I, on the other hand can be obsessed with any of the following: popcorn (non-natural and highly flavoured), potato chips, ice-cream, chocolate, sweets etc. Do you see the difference here and how it would translate to the hips?

In the past I have dieted with Weight Watchers and achieved great results. Unfortunately my maintenance follow-up was not so great. Rather than continue on with my healthy eating, I would assume that once I was skinny, I would just stay that way. Sadly, that is never the case. By slipping back into my old habits, the weight would creep back on and the 5kg (11 pounds) I had been so diligent about saying Au Revoir to, was back with me. Bonjour! it would say.

We all know that the idealistic French woman (and indeed many real ones) are very disciplined with their caloric intake, thus ensuring they stay their ideal weight and are making the most of their lovely clothes, which are all the same size, not varying from 10 up to 12-14 as mine are.

Even though I said to myself 'no more Weight Watchers' after finding it too restrictive, I yet again found myself turning up to a Weight Watchers meeting near work. I decided that I would try the new points programme and told myself I would continue going to meetings until I reached my goal weight of 57-60kg (125 to 132 pounds). I was over 70kg (154 pounds) at the time.

Clearly I needed a little external discipline to help me along as I hadn't lost anything myself. And if I had, it was back. Now, I don't buy this 'perhaps that's the weight you are naturally' business. Not for me anyway. I could shovel in all sorts of crap foods. Sweet or salty snack foods are designed to make you want more. And I wasn't happy with how I felt or how my clothes (the ones I could fit) looked.

I have found that you can train your palate, and that the more you have of something, the more you want of it, whether that something is a big, crunchy, plain salad, or a large bag of jellybeans. Even knowing this, and knowing how those two things make me feel (one, vibrant, alive and quenched, the other, a hot headache and craving for sugar) didn't help me make good decisions all the time.

Rather than rebelling against discipline, I have decided to look at it like money. If you spend more than you earn, you go into debt. In my younger years I did just that, but for many years now I've happily had savings building up, and not many problems resisting purchasing temptation.

Not so with food. Obviously I regularly went into debt with food and drink, and had the not-so-chic figure to show for it. I now look at my Weight Watchers points as a budget to spend. And so I won't go hungry or over-spend, I have to use it wisely.

I can happily report that the new Weight Watchers programme is working really well for me, and seems much easier to stick to for the long term. I can have mini blow-outs every week if I want (and I usually do) and still decrease on the scales. This is the way to keep me interested. If it's not fun, I don't want to know about it.

I never attended meetings before, so that may be helping too. By saying to myself I am committed to attending until I am a certain weight, meant if I didn't want to waste my money, I'd better do something about it.

I am happy to let you know I am now 6-7kg (13-15 pounds) lighter than I was, and at least halfway to my goal. I have had to buy a few new items of clothing, because my jeans are falling off me. Some have been put away to get rid of as they are ridiculously huge, and some I am able to cinch in with a belt for now. These are the same jeans that I formerly could not sit in for more than five minutes at a time.

So I guess the purpose of this essay is to face the fear and do it anyway. My fear was if I wrote about my weight loss, I would jinx it once again. Now I know this is silly. The books I have been reading lately, old books I have had for a long time (a few listed below) reminded me that *I make up my mind, I make my reality*.

I wrote down a quote the other day which really spoke to me:

'*I know what I like, I know what I don't like. I know the way I want to live, and I make it happen that way*'. – Anthea Turner

And some more 'current' (they're all really quite vintage in age) reading:

Inspiring Messages for Daily Living by Dr Norman Vincent Peale

Seeds of Greatness by Denis Waitley

10 Days to a Great New Life by William E. Edwards

The Power of Positive Thinking by Dr Norman Vincent Peale (I've been listening to the audiobook in the car)

None of them are about weight and slimness, but they all encourage me to be better in all areas of my life, including being svelte.

More on slimming

'French women appreciate that Rome wasn't built in a day (and neither was France), but rather 'little by little'. The progress of your life towards peak experiences in all aspects of living will take time.

Changes made drastically or all at once are often the sorts of modifications that don't stick. Like New Year's resolutions, they are upheld proudly for a little while, but then we fall back to our old ways. Arrive at your new ways gradually, and you will leave your old ways too far behind for easy return.

And if you slip up a bit, you won't feel a failure; you will know how to get back on track because it isn't all or nothing. It's a game of inches.'

- Mireille Guiliano, French Women For All Seasons

This is how I am thinking about my weight loss journey. I arrived at the halfway mark pretty promptly and directly, and have been having a more relaxing time of it for quite a few weeks now. I feel ready to tackle the second half.

I love being more svelte, of my clothes looking much better than they used to, of my legs looking slimmer and my stomach looking (a little) flatter. I love that I feel sexier and more like the chic Parisian femme I know I am in my mind. I love looking like someone who gives a damn and cares about what they look like (I didn't often feel like that when I couldn't fit my clothes).

But I have been ignoring my Weight Watchers tracker book for more days than I have written in it though, and as a result have found myself on the slippery upwards slope by a kilo or two.

I am keen to carry on becoming my most ideal self weight-wise. One thing I do know is that writing everything down that you eat and drink definitely helps if you're wanting to slim down. It might be via a method like Weight Watchers or you might just jot down what you consume and in what quantities. All Weight Watchers does is help you know the 'price' of things.

You could do it after the fact or before, by planning out what you're going to have for breakfast, lunch, dinner and morning and afternoon tea that that day. Getting into this habit will help redirect and refine what you eat. Planning ahead is the best way, but even knowing I'm going to be making a note of what I'm eating will help me be aware of it.

Sometimes I'll eat 'whatever' anyway, but on writing it down, I realise it can be accommodated in the day, if most other things are healthy. Isn't that how our French sisters do it?

Last night I wrote out my to-do list for today. The first item on my list is 'Be slim'. Normally my lists are a little more practical but why not be whimsical for once.

First thing in the morning, whilst waiting for the kettle to boil for tea to sip in bed with the Sunday paper (one of life's little pleasures), I read a few pages from *French Women For All Seasons*.

It was enough to get me back into my chic mindset and look forward to being disciplined with my diet as a pleasure and enjoyable, rather than that I am depriving myself.

I love it when that happens.

The secret to permanent slimness?

I've had a bit of an epiphany with my food choices lately, and some helpful resources I came across at just the right time have been the catalyst.

From my mid-twenties I've joined Weight Watchers a few times and followed their very sensible diet but always fell off eventually, then went back to how I ate before and put the weight back on.

We're not talking about dozens of kilos here but the same 5-10kg (11-22 pounds) which were quite inconvenient when it came to feeling chic and healthy and looking good.

I've always considered myself to have a sweet tooth and I'd tell myself it was relatively harmless really to have sweet treats and if they were low-fat then there was little chance for damage. That's the old low-fat/high-carb dietary way of thinking that has had me brainwashed from back in the nineties (or was it eighties?).

The 'diets don't work' message we've all heard before confused me too. If I said to myself 'right, I'm not going to follow a diet, I'm going to eat what I want', I *would* eat what I wanted, regardless of if it was healthy or not. And of course I put on weight. So if I'm not going to go on a diet, and I'm going to not go on a diet, what do I do?

One day several months ago I searched for a link between sugar consumption and sinus headaches. I realised that I would invariably wake up with one after a 'treat' night of sugary crap. I came upon some research confirming this which horrified me. It made such disgusting reading that I gave up eating sugar for the most part from then on.

I'm not totally 100% strict, I'll always join in something when we're out for dinner etc. But I just don't, for the most part, buy sweet things for myself at home now. I keep myself from feeling deprived by saying I can have anything I like, as long as it's not sugary.

But from eliminating the bulk of sugar from my diet, everything started falling into place. I naturally wanted more nutritious food, I felt better and had more energy, I slept better and my weight started dropping. From a stable weight in the late sixties (kg that is, or 148-149 pounds), I am now around 64kg (141 pounds) and I know there is a little bit still to come off (I'm 5 foot 7 or 170cm so 135 pounds/61kg is meant to be ideal for my height).

When the weight stops coming off then that will be my natural weight. I am not measuring portions because you don't really need to when it's real food you're eating. I know that 1-2 pieces of fruit is a good amount to eat, or half a chicken breast is right for me, etc.

After starting on my non-sugar thing, I came across a book at the Red Cross shop for $2 which I almost left on the shelf. I opened it up though and read a few pages, and it was talking about cutting out sugar and how this was the key to being slim and healthy. I thought 'we're on the same wave-length', so I bought the book and I have to say it's the best $2 I've ever spent. The book is by Lee Janogly and called *'Only Fat People Skip Breakfast'*. Lee is an English author who is a diet counsellor and every page is filled with common sense, humour and good ideas.

This book did for me with food what Alan Carr's book did for me with alcohol (see my 'How I Became a Non-Drinker' article in Chapter 4 of this book). It really changed my mindset towards the foods I chose and makes me feel happy with those choices. Coincidentally I think the reason why I am so happy being a non-drinker now is the same reason I feel so well not taking in much sugar, as alcohol has tons of sugar in it.

Two other books which I have also gained lots of good information and inspiration from are:

Peter Walsh – *'Does This Clutter Make My Butt Look Fat'*. I love Peter for his decluttering motivation, but this book is even better – decluttering with weight loss in mind. As with his other books Peter has lots of common sense and good practical ideas you can immediately put into practice.

Gary Taubes - *'Why We Get Fat (And What To Do About It)'*. Gary explains the scientific background on why we are getting fatter and I find that really helps make habit changes that stick. It's one thing to be told what to do, but it's quite another to understand why it is good for you to eat something and not another. This book sounds boring but it's really not.

Here is what a typical day of food looks like for me now.

Breakfast:

1-2 pieces fresh fruit, washed and sliced – I eat whatever is in season/on special/what looks good at the supermarket or fruit shop.

Small handful of mixed raw nuts (about 16-20) – sometimes I buy a mixed bag and sometimes I buy bags of a single type and mix my own. If I do this I might have 2 brazils, 6 almonds, 4 cashews, 2 hazels, 2 macadamias, 2 pecans for example

A **couple of dessert-spoons of yoghurt** on top (mostly but not always) – my favoured yoghurt is full-fat with the only ingredients being milk and culture.

This gets me through to mid-morning when I have a **soy or milk café latte**.

At lunch-time, I have a **Giant Salad**. My lunch salad deserves capital letters. I use a pasta dish (not the family dish, the individual dish) and I pile in fresh salad ingredients, add some protein (half a cooked chicken breast, tuna in springwater or any leftover roast meat from dinner, diced on top) and my favourite treat – creamy dressing. Currently my favourites are Paul Newman – Ranch or Creamy Caesar. I don't have any bread or carbs with my lunch salad and I don't really miss it.

Mid- to late-afternoon I will have a **small snack**, maybe a few slices of cheese on crackers, but more often than not I will steal some of my husband's protein powder and have a quick protein drink. That stops me coming home starving and looking for pre-dinner snacks.

Then dinner is usually **meat and vegetables**, the old-fashioned way. A roast or mini-roast in the oven with roast pumpkin and carrot (with potato maybe twice a week) and steamed veges dressed with olive oil (such as broccoli, cauliflower etc). And some packet or home-made gravy. Sometimes we have a stir-fry. Two or three times a month we'll have a pasta dish.

My father-in-law is from England, and he went through sugar rationing during the second-world war. To this day he doesn't have a sweet tooth and couldn't care less about dessert, chocolate or anything like that. And he's pretty lean and healthy for his age of seventy-nine.

Better late than never I say, and my 'sweet enough without sugar' chic and slender lifestyle starts now. Come with me – are you brave enough to try?

Chapter 13.
The French approach to exercise

Even though I like to feel good and look even better, I've never been a fan of exercise. It's too much effort, you have to put special clothes on, you often have to drive somewhere to do it and all this really eats into your precious time.

So for a long time I never did any, and you know where that got me (out of shape and with no energy). Read on to discover how I turned this situation around, and now I rarely go a day without moving my body, *and* incredibly, I actually look forward to it. Truly!

Moving like a French woman

In Mireille Guiliano's fabulous book *French Women Don't Get Fat* she makes some interesting points about French women and exercise in chapter ten 'Moving like a French woman'.

Mireille says traditional exercise where you change into your workout gear doesn't go with being French. She describes it as a great, joyless effort cutting two hours out of your day to travel, change, learning and waiting to use machines, showering, drying your hair and so on. And you have to pay for it. I couldn't have written it better myself. She describes exactly why I am not a gym bunny anymore.

She also mentions an 'overheated' workout can do the opposite for you than a milder exertion. It revs up your appetite so you eat more afterwards. And if you decide all that energy expenditure is just too much to put up with, you quit. It can encourage the 'all or nothing' mindset.

I couldn't agree more. I remember some particularly high-energy aerobics classes when I left the gym on a Saturday morning literally shaking. And I was ravenously hungry. My poor body, all churned up. And then I looked around for the nearest horse to eat...

I think it comes down to what suits you. Some people thrive on high-energy workouts but I know for myself they are counter-productive to my health and tranquillity. I much prefer gentle exercise as part of how I live my life.

Walking outside either at a fast-paced clip or a leisurely meander depending on my mood, how much time I have and whether I feel tired or energised is my favourite form of exercise. I also feel really fortunate that I have found an enjoyable yoga class to add to my walking.

My yoga teacher echoed my walking philosophy in one of her talks. She said you will have days when you have lots of energy and feel great, and days when you feel tired and want to be more gentle on yourself.

In the past I've felt guilty if I've had a 'slack' gym workout and either pushed myself to try harder or left the gym feeling guilty because I didn't take full advantage of my workout time. Now how much fun does that sound? Again, it's down to the individual – there are plenty of people who enjoy the high-octane effort of a gym workout, but I'm not one of them.

My husband and I have had this conversation a few times – he knows how much I enjoy my gentle pursuits of walking and yoga, and he's told me how much enjoyment he gets from his hard-out cardio and weights gym sessions four to five times per week.

In her book, Mireille encourages us to increase our walking by adding regular 'dedicated' walks to our day. Start small and make smart strolls a part of each day. It could be walking part way to work (I drive, but often walk to the bank, post office or library during the day. When I worked in the city I would use my lunch hour to walk from the bottom of town to the top to visit the library or just for a stroll) or walking for twenty minutes after dinner to aid digestion and wind down before bed.

Of course you won't want to wear stilettos, but you don't have to wear chunky sports shoes either. There are many styles of comfortable flats which allow you to be comfortable and look good in your normal day clothes too.

When I travelled to London, I had a number of days where I was a sightseeing group of one. It was lovely to have the day to myself, and still have friends to meet up with at night (they were working). One of the days I caught the tube to Chelsea/Sloane Square area and just walked around imagining I lived in one of the gorgeous pastel coloured terrace houses. I eventually made my way to a shopping area and another tube station where I rode back to my friend's home later in the afternoon. Not a typical touristy outing but I've always enjoyed seeing how people live, and not just gawping through the gates of Buckingham Palace (although I did that too of course).

I've done this a few times in my own city. The area we live in is pretty boring and out of the way and not really suitable for walking, but I can drive to a lovely, older area and park the car. Then the plan is to walk as if I lived there and enjoy the beautiful homes, perhaps stop in a cafe or window-shop. Enjoyable exercise is what I'm all about.

Gaining more energy

Let me tell you about the time I joined an outdoor fitness group in my search for enjoyable exercise.

This unusual behaviour was prompted by a customer who is also a fitness trainer (he used to train me when I went to the gym quite a few years ago). He now runs his own outdoor fitness company and invited me to join a ten-week programme, for free. He's such a great guy and said 'just come along, join in'. The class was in a public park a two-minute walk from work, so I had no excuses.

There were eleven other people in the group and we did all sorts of mad things. We were instructed to *run up a mountain*. I had to walk/run most of the way, but I still got there. It brought home to me just how unfit I am. Walking and yoga, as much as I love them, don't get your heart rate up.

I had a little bit of a headache at the top of the mountain, and had visions of me all burnt out and shaky like after a full-on aerobics workout, but I will just take it easy and know my limits.

The class was held twice a week. I'm so happy that I was offered the opportunity to try this class as I would *never* have gone looking for it on my own. It reminded me how much I enjoy running and exerting myself. It's such a pleasure to exercise outside too. I just can't get excited about being inside a gym, walking nowhere on a treadmill.

After my shower when I arrived home I was like a jellyfish. It felt *so* good. I slept the sleep of the dead too.

So, did I keep up the outdoor fitness training? Well, no I did not. I don't mind telling you it wasn't my dream exercise scenario. My husband told me after the course finished that he was surprised I even went once. He knows me so well. I realised when I did this class that I'd been missing some high energy workouts, which do make you feel really good.

I had been doing yoga and walking which was more like strolling. Inspired by my high energy outdoor workouts, I have introduced faster walking into my days (ooh, pulling out all the stops Fiona, I hear you say). Some days if I don't feel like going for a walk I tell myself 'just walk as slow as you like and go the shorter route' and other days when I'm full of beans I go the longer route, really fast.

And, my favourite part of all, I can go any time I like, and walking is portable. I don't need to drive there, and I don't need to be there at a certain time. That's really important to me.

How to make walking fun

I made the best purchase last year which I am beyond thrilled with. Before I go into that though I want to tell you about me and exercise. I'm not a fan. If it's gentle, I'm happy. But sometimes even then I can't be bothered which is not a very chic way to think I know. I love my yoga class when I'm there but if there's a reason I can't go, I'm not unhappy about it.

Same with walking, in my mind I am a walker and true, I will happily walk into town (which takes about thirty to forty minutes) rather than take the bus or car, but walking daily for exercise like I 'think' I do, well it gets blown off rather often.

I never took our iPod out walking because it's quite big, I need a pocket because I was afraid of dropping it and also because I never remembered to. Plus, I like to work things out in my head whilst walking and music seemed to intrude on that.

Then I had an idea to get a tiny cheap iPod and put only my podcasts/ audiobooks/ saved audio clips etc on, as I love listening to them for inspiration. I listen to them when I'm getting ready in the morning, driving in the car, and in the evening when I wash my face. If I bought a tiny cheap iPod I could listen to my inspiring podcasts more and actually look forward to walking!

So I bought an iPod Shuffle 2GB and it's SO tiny. The size of an inch-square piece of Lindt chocolate tiny. Ridiculously tiny. But it fits all the podcasts I'd ever want to listen to, and has a little springy clip on the back, so it attaches to my neckline or bra strap and I'm off.

The first day I used it I planned to walk for around thirty minutes, but chose to go down extra streets simply because I wanted to keep listening. I ended up walking for fifty minutes and it seemed effortless. And the next day an hour. Yay!

Even today, several months later I realise I have walked most days since I bought it. And I still am keen to go out walking and listening, the novelty hasn't worn off.

Now I totally understand all those people I keep seeing with earphones in (which used to be everyone except me). I'm not a technology person, I don't have a smart phone yet for example, but I totally love it when technology offers me a simple, fun and inexpensive solution. And I can still hear traffic over the talking so I am safe (plus I always look when crossing the roads).

Working on my mind and body at the same time – love it!

And the unexpected bonus is that I have been using it when I do my housework too, and don't mind pottering away cleaning our home. I paid NZ$69 for ours, and I see they are US$49 in America. What a bargain for such a handy device.

Here are some of my favourite inspirational listenings:

- Tonya Leigh's blog post audio clips (plus her YouTube soirees – I save them as audio using an online converter then save them to my iPod Shuffle)

- The Simple Sophisticate podcasts on iTunes

- Interviews with inspiring people as found on iTunes (such as Peter Walsh, Louise Hay and Brian Tracy)

PS. Promise this is *not* a paid advertisement…but it should be.

Chapter 14.
Breakfast, Lunch and Dinner

My favourite chic breakfast

One of my favourite breakfasts is poached egg on toast. It is nutritious, delicious and keeps me going until lunchtime.

I used to make it in an egg poaching pan we have which has four little cups, one for each egg. If ever there was a one-trick-pony it's that pan. It's very quick and useful, but I never felt chic eating an egg which was moulded into a perfect round shape, like a jelly. And I had to use an aerosol oil spray to coat the non-stick surface beforehand.

I just couldn't imagine my ideal French girl Sabine using that pan or spray oil in her Paris apartment!

So I simplified to a small saucepan, in which I pour boiling water and a dash of malt vinegar (if you don't already know, a tiny amount of vinegar helps the egg white emulsify quickly for a more successful poached egg).

I'd also just like to say please use free-range eggs. I can't bear the thought of those hard-working little chickens crammed into cages. They deserve better than that. It always makes me sad when I see battery eggs in folks supermarket trolleys.

Free-range eggs look a lot healthier too – they have bright orange/yellow yolks.

Once the water is on a rolling boil I crack in an egg. After a broken yolk disaster and advice from a cafe-owner friend I now open the egg into a small dish and have it waiting. Every so often if the yolk breaks I then have scrambled eggs (better to have it break in a dish, than in boiling water).

What I also do before the egg meets the water (like 'the rubber hits the road', but the kitchen version) is to swirl the water around like a whirlpool with a spoon. Then, when the egg is introduced, all the white starts wrapping around the yolk to make a lovely round bundle, just like you would receive in a cafe.

Oh, and use a deep pot rather than a flat pan to poach with. Have the toast waiting, as it's only a minute or two before the egg is done (I take it out with a big holey spoon as soon as the white looks done, and the egg yolk is still beautifully runny).

I often ask cafe staff what their secrets are and they are always happy to share. One of the chefs from my favourite cafe was shopping in our store once and when he said where he worked I fell all over him - 'what's the secret to your scrambled eggs there?' I asked. 'Lots of cream and butter', he replied. So when I'm having a more treat-y breakfast I always add a dash of cream to my scrambled eggs and cook them in a little bit of butter.

But back to my poached egg breakfast. Whereas scrambled eggs require two eggs and a dash of cream (so a few more calories), I can happily exist all morning on one egg poached, on a piece of lightly buttered whole-grain toast (Vogels is great bread available here, it's very dense and heavy, chock-full of seeds and grains, and the slices are a lot smaller in size. Nice and chewy too).

Lately I have been tearing up a few basil leaves over the plated egg/toast since our herb pot is growing well. Fresh parsley snipped over the top would be delicious also. The touch of green looks *very* designer-y. A sprinkle of salt and a crunch of black pepper and it is a dish that would do Sabine proud.

And of course breakfast is not complete without a cafe au lait. I make mine with a shot of strong coffee (brewed in a Bialetti) topped up with milk, then microwaved hot. If I run out of real coffee, I make a very strong coffee with a teaspoon of freeze-dried coffee and a tiny amount of hot water, then top up and microwave as before.

Bon appetit.

Chic lunches

Lunch is often a real problem area for me. I just don't know what to have! When I come across (or in this case think up) a great lunch I am tempted to start a 'Fifi's Menu note-book' with meal ideas. It would have to be something I could imagine myself dining on in my Paris apartment of course.

Here is one of my 'Paris Lunches' I dreamed up:

Warm Pumpkin Salad

Roast in a pan at moderate heat (180C or 350F):

Small dice of pumpkin

Onion chopped into chunks

A few garlic cloves crushed

Big pieces of capsicum, and

Fresh rosemary using a drizzle of olive oil and a tiny drizzle of balsamic vinegar.

The balsamic caramelises and is a lot more mellow than when used in a dressing. I planned to add pumpkin seeds also but forgot. Next time!

When the roast mix was cooked I stirred through a small-ish amount of cooked brown rice and topped with torn basil leaves and a sprinkling of grated gouda cheese. Then a grind of salt and fresh black pepper.

This recipe can be served hot, warm or cold. The acid test of course is can I imagine Sabine eating this in her apartment or a cafe. Yes I can. And, it was delicious.

On my mid-week day off work my husband takes our sole car to work, so I either have to drop him in and pick him up, or be organised food-wise for a day at home. There is nothing I like more than a day at home so I very rarely want the car.

I always am organised the day before with dinner provisions, but often forget about lunch. The ingredients for my warm salad above were all in the pantry/fridge/herb pots and dictated the flavours somewhat.

To the roast mix you could also add any or all of carrots, beetroot, kumara (sweet potato) and potato - make them all the same size dice. Any herbs could be used - sturdy ones in the roast mix, leafy, delicate ones at the end. The brown rice could become cous cous and you could add any type of cheese, meat or canned fish for protein.

From Anne Barone's book *Chic & Slim - Encore* I loved her version of Tabouli which I used to make a lot for lunch, but haven't in a while. Revisiting her books reminded me of that recipe and my warm salad lunch was born.

Tomorrow, back at work I plan to use the leftover baked pumpkin mix over lettuce, with a bit of cold brown rice and other raw salad ingredients. The cooked caramelised component really adds a bit of *je ne sais quoi* to the basic raw salad. Ooh la la!

La baguette

Few images are as quintessentially French as the baguette. When I buy a baguette I always get a jaunty Frenchness to my step, and feel quite chic when I break a piece off at home. But invariably I eat some, enjoy, eat a bit more, become full and then leave the rest to go hard overnight.

I have decided to make the baguette a more regular part of my life, as I always feel more stylish breaking up a chunk than pulling a slice of square bread out of a plastic bag. What I do now is:

a) buy the baguette (yes I could learn to make them, but my breadmaking has turned out a little doughy for my taste so baking them is for another day when I'm in the mood to experiment) and then,

b) slice into 10cm/4 inch pieces.

The baguettes I most recently bought had exactly six per loaf. I then freeze them in a ziplock bag (after enjoying that day's piece fresh). The day I want a piece I take it from the freezer, either in the morning, or at a pinch half an hour before I want it. They thaw very quickly at room temperature and if you've frozen them on the day of purchase they taste almost as good.

I have mostly been having them for lunch, either as is alongside a complete ('with protein') salad or split in half and both flat sides covered in something if having a side salad (raw veges and salad ingredients, no protein). Two 'somethings' I have enjoyed lately are:

An egg, hardboiled and fork mashed with a small dollop of Best Foods mayo and capers, or

A small portion of cold roast-chicken, cut up fine and mixed with the same small dollop of Best Foods mayo and finely diced raw celery.

Top with a crunch of black pepper.

It's nice to have the bread always handy, and even though the portions seem to have shrunk in the freezer since I cut them (and I thought to myself 'should I have two?') I have only ever had the one piece, and never thought afterwards 'I'm still hungry'. I'm always perfectly sated. Portion control! It works!

The other night when I reheated the rest of a pasta bake and served it with a salad dressed with equal parts extra virgin olive oil and balsamic vinegar, my husband, whose favourite thing in the world is bread but doesn't often have it said, 'do you have some bread in the freezer?' When I placed the baguette down in front of him (resisting saying 'Et voila) he remarked that our table looked very Italian, and that the bread in the picture looked like it completed the meal.

If I was Sabine, living in my Paris apartment, with a boulangerie on the corner which I passed each night on my way home from the Metro station, then I would buy a half-baguette and eat it fresh. I can pretend that's me when I have my piece of baguette with lunch and it actually has made me feel more chic all day.

That's what it's about for me, adding in little touches of chic Frenchness to my life, and this in turn encourages me to act chicly (in all ways, not just with food).

Best. Soup. Ever.

It's a bold statement I know. There are a number of reasons (and this is my sales pitch on) why this is the best soup ever.

- Quick and easy to make

- Frugal

- Lots of nutrition - brightly coloured vegetables and good amount of protein

- Low in fat/calories

- Delicious

The recipe came from *New Zealand House & Garden* magazine many, many years ago. Since then I have made it a lot (my mother is the soup queen and I think I have inherited this gene thankfully). It has an ingredient list that can be memorised easily, and I make different versions of it for variety of flavour, and to use up fading vegetables.

Here is the original version:

- 1 brown onion, chopped and sautéed in a little olive oil

- 1 400g (14 oz) can of plain or flavoured chopped tomatoes and juice

- 1 cup red lentils (rinsed and picked over – take out the odd yucky looking one)

- 4 cups/1 litre/1 quart chicken stock (or any other stock flavour you like). I use a mix of my homemade chicken stock and store-bought stock powder/cubes.

Also, all the basic recipe ingredients are 'store cupboard ingredients' - I always have them on hand.

Bring to the boil and simmer for 20 minutes.

This soup has been my staple lunch at work for this past, and many other winters. It reheats beautifully in the microwave. I have even been known to make it before work (when I really have no extra time). The really quick version involves throwing the onion into the other ingredients without sautéing and then cooking for twenty minutes. If you were really pressed for time you could use the stock, a can of flavoured tomatoes and the red lentils, no onion.

My current batch, which was extra tasty, involves a handful of fresh pumpkin cubes. These cook within the time frame and I just break up the pieces with a potato masher when done. It's a nicer soup a little rustic than pureed smooth. I also added fresh oregano (just tore the leaves off the stem once washed) from my garden pot, dried sweet basil and six bay leaves (which are removed after cooking).

Other additions that are good:

- As I said before, any tired vegetables can be chopped up small (since you're not pureeing) and added

- Fresh or dried herbs

- A little tomato paste

- Any cooked meats if you like, however the lentils provide good protein, so not needed for a balanced meal

- If you have any, a dollop of full fat plain unsweetened yoghurt added just before serving is divine, as is Parmesan. Yum

- Different flavoured tomatoes or spices for a different type - Italian, Mexican, Indian

I also made an Indian version including pumpkin as above, but with Indian flavoured chopped tomatoes and an extra teaspoon of yellow curry powder. I used dried soup mix rather than red lentils. Dried soup mix contains red lentils, barley, split peas etc. It needs to be cooked for an hour and a half rather than the twenty minutes for red lentils only. I think this Indian version is my favourite yet.

I also rarely make the single batch. Doubling the quantities doesn't take much more effort, and I often freeze the second container for an instant weeks' worth of lunches. I either eat this by itself, or with bread, or cheese on toast.

I am a big fan of slow food and slow cooking, but this is my favourite 'fast food' recipe.

Bon appétit!

Comfort food for a Sunday evening

Sunday evenings to me spell something comforting in the kitchen. Often this means a casserole in the slow cooker, or an Italian dish. Last night I made a pasta bake which I am in the process of perfecting. Of course the fact that I like to use up what I have in the pantry means it will not taste identical every time, but perfecting the base recipe is my goal.

I can also make it less carb- and sauce-heavy than a traditional pasta bake. I don't use that much pasta in it, add lots of vegetables and use cottage cheese instead of béchamel or ricotta. Cottage cheese still tastes delicious but is low in fat and high in protein. This probably makes up for the amount of mozzarella I use.

It is comfort food, but it also means I can compile everything in one dish, put it in the oven for an hour or two and sit down with the Sunday papers. The aroma as it cooks is lovely too.

Here is my recipe:

In the deep lasagne or casserole dish add the following in layers (you don't need to worry about greasing or oiling the dish, just pile everything in).

Mix together in a big bowl the bottom layer then add to dish:

- Diced pumpkin (about 1 inch cubes)
- Silver beet (chard), washed and chopped
- One onion, chopped
- 1-2 cloves garlic, crushed and chopped
- 500g (about 1 lb) cottage cheese
- Seasoning - plenty of salt and pepper, and this time I used sweet smoked paprika, chicken stock powder, dried chilli flakes and rubbed sage

With the first layer you can use any vegetables you want to use up. I always include pumpkin as it imparts a rich sweetness and thickens the pasta bake. You can use a small container of cottage cheese if it's a smaller dish you have. I ended up with servings enough for six, not two.

Second layer, sprinkle mozzarella cheese and then add dried, uncooked pasta. I see no point in having to cook pasta first. I am essentially a lazy (sorry, efficient) cook. You can use lasagne sheets, but all I had was macaroni elbows and they worked just fine. Use enough to cover the cheese in a single layer.

Third layer, pour a can or two of diced tomatoes over, spreading out the tomato pieces. Rinse out the can(s) with the tiniest amount of water and pour this in too. This time I added a splash of red wine (just into the middle of the mix, and let it soak in) as I thought there might have not been quite enough liquid in the mix. You don't want too much liquid though, just enough to absorb into the pasta.

Fourth and final layer, add another generous sprinkle of mozzarella cheese. Parmesan would be good too, if you have any (we didn't). Then breadcrumbs. You can use store-bought breadcrumbs or homemade. Since my sister gave us as a gift the wonderful Cuisinart mini food processor I haven't bought breadcrumbs. I save the crusts from bread in the freezer and thaw a few whenever I want crumbs. Place them (torn up) into the food processor, add a clove or two of garlic and any seasoning you might like and blitz. The garlic tastes amazing in them.

Sprinkle breadcrumbs on the top (hopefully you haven't reached the rim of the dish) and place in a moderate 180 C (350 F) oven for at least 1 1/2 hours. I didn't cover mine at all last night, but next time perhaps I would for the first half of the cooking time. The crumbs weren't burnt, but they were quite crispy after the full cooking time.

When you want to check that it is ready, stick a fork in and check that the pumpkin is soft, and try a piece of the pasta to check it is cooked.

Bon appetit!

Enjoying cooking at home

I am often asked about eating well and cooking at home, and sometimes it seems like magic to these people that I can serve a roast dinner up. Hearing this makes me think back to when I was younger and had just left home at around nineteen, having never really cooked a dinner. But I started out with what I liked to eat and practised cooking those dishes.

There were some disasters such as serving canned pumpkin soup which I thought I'd make more homemade by adding garlic. Did I mention it was raw garlic that I stirred through the heated soup? It did not go down well, literally. And I can't believe I used canned pumpkin soup either, with pumpkins being so inexpensive and easy to turn into a delicious soup. But I was learning.

I also made my first (and only so far) batch of scones many years ago which turned out like little rocks. I threw them on the lawn, but even the birds could not get their beaks through them. As far as baking goes I've stuck with muffins and slices. Who knows though, maybe I'll try scones again someday?

So I started out by trial and error, and gradually gained confidence and knowledge in the kitchen. I'm still not a fancy cook and don't create loads of dishes, but the ones I do often, I do well. I'm not a total food purist either. I use a packet mix here and there to add flavour to a casserole or an instant gravy. I find people who say they would 'never eat anything not made from scratch' quite tiresome and preachy. But that's just me.

Having said that, I have been trialling lately how to add flavour and thickness to a casserole without a packet mix, and making my own gravy from the pan drippings. I have a notebook where I write my makeshift recipes down. That way if it's tasty and receives rave reviews, I can remember what I put in for next time. It's just a cheap little school notebook so I don't mind scribbling down ideas on the go or getting it too near the food.

If you eat out a lot and want to eat in more, I would suggest you think about the dishes you like to order when you dine out and then try to recreate them at home. I often think diet makeover programmes fall over in that respect. They take a family who is used to eating fast food burgers and chips every night and try to force them into stir-fry and miso soup. If I was the food expert, I would take their favourite meal and show them how to make it at home.

Say if they ate fast-food burger and fries every night. Imagine instead good-quality fresh bread burger buns, homemade lean mince patties with chopped onion, herbs and seasonings (which can be made ahead of time and maybe frozen, for an instant component of the meal for busy evenings), fresh lettuce pieces and tomato slices, a slice of real cheese, and a blob of good quality mayo.

You could serve this with hot fries made by slicing scrubbed, unpeeled potatoes into wedges and oven baking them in a smear or spray of oil, along with salt and pepper, seasonings or herbs sprinkled over.

So that's my thought – think about your favourite dine-in or take-out meals and write them down, then have a go at recreating them at home. Yes, you might have some disasters, but it will be fun, and the satisfaction of producing a meal in your own kitchen is immense. Even after all these years of cooking I feel really proud of myself when I try something new and my husband goes on about how good it is.

Make up your own 'home menu' to choose from. For I often find it's coming up with the idea for dinner that is the most challenging thing. If I had a menu of favourites, old and new, I could simply choose. Wouldn't that be luxurious?

Chapter 15.
On good health

'Good health' and 'healthy living' can seem such boring subjects. Until, that is, you don't have good health. Then there is nothing more important in the world. Good health is something many of us take for granted until we lose it (hopefully temporarily), I know I certainly have. I have also realised that once you pass the age of forty, you ignore your health at your peril.

Our bodies can put up with a lot, but at some stage all our unhealthy habits are going to catch up with us. I find it helpful to think of my body as my best friend and constant companion in this life – because she is! And I like to look after my best friend. I want to make sure she is happy, she has good food to eat, and that she gets adequate rest. It's the least I can do.

A health schedule

I have been thinking lately about how I can be more pro-active about my health. Now that I am 'forty plus' I want to not take my health for granted. I plan to live a long, healthy, happy and vibrant life.

To address the 'healthy' part of the equation I have always been interested in good nutrition, and including incidental exercise in your day etc. The other side of things though is medical check-ups, and catching something that might start out small but if not detected could be a big problem later on.

I had a mole on my leg removed privately a couple of years back because it bothered me. More than one medical professional, including a skin surgeon told me it was nothing to worry about. When the results came back it was a melanoma. I had one more surgery to take surrounding tissue, and thankfully it had not spread.

This scary incident taught me to trust my own instincts, but also now I have a twice a year skin check. My skin Doctor sends me a letter every six months and when I see it in the mail I think 'is it really six months already?' and then get around to ringing him for an appointment and then it's another four weeks before I can see him.

The one car that my husband and I share, without fail has its service every July when its warrant of fitness is due. I actually make sure that happens but I let my own appointments slide, and a car is certainly more replaceable than a body.

Yes, health appointments can be quite bothersome and cost money too, but I have now made a decision to 'just do it'. Book them in and go. Don't think about if I 'want to', because who ever does?

To assist myself in this I have made up a schedule so that I know when I have to book myself in for.

September – full Doctor check-up

October and April – skin checks

March – full dental check-up

In New Zealand, it's only recommended that a woman has a smear test every three years, but about ten years ago a Doctor I visited said he recommended annually to his patients, as sometimes the results weren't that clear, and if you only went every three years, it could be six years between readings and he considered that too long.

I also had my first mammogram a year or two ago. In New Zealand they start being covered by the public health system at age forty five. I received a letter well before that though, saying an appointment had been made for me. When I arrived, having paid the exorbitant parking fee and then waiting for half an hour, I was told that a mistake was made and the mammogram was meant for someone else.

Yes really. I was quite speechless. And they told me I could go. I said to them 'I've taken time off work and paid the parking fee, can I please have a mammogram even if it was meant for someone else (because they weren't there, it was an empty appointment), and I'm only a few years off forty five (that was stretching it). They eventually relented and I had one (it was fine). What a crazy morning that was, but at least I got to have a mammogram, even if it was by mistake.

My current Doctor also recommended I add an eye check-up to my list, not only for seeing, but also for eye health. I read in a magazine that every two years is recommended and that some optometrists have special machines that check the eye very thoroughly.

So apart from scheduling in my reminders to make appointments each year is to investigate an optometrist to go and see.

I feel really good about making a schedule and making the appointments myself to do something in a certain month. By not waiting for the reminder letters:

a) I am not relying on them to remember - sometimes reminder letters are lost or not sent out.

b) I don't begrudge the appointment because I am the one that has made it.

I think I have all things covered, and I feel really good about my new planned health schedule.

How I became a non-drinker

We all make our own decisions in life and I don't want to presume to influence yours, however I'm often asked about being a non-drinker so here is my story. I think there are a lot of very normal people out there who are not happy with the way they think about drink. I know I wasn't.

Never in a million years would I have considered myself to have a drinking problem or need to go to AA (I still don't), however I would jokingly say I was concerned at how much I looked forward to a glass of Chardonnay, brandy and dry or gin and tonic when I got home.

I also did not like the fact that these drinks helped me keep me just that little bit fatter than I would have liked. This is due to the fact that alcohol is highly calorific being worse than pure sugar, plus you might add mixers (choose your poison – sugar or artificial sweeteners). And a drink seems to include snacks for me.

So I had a love/hate relationship with my cocktail hour. Love the chance to sit down with a magazine or book, hate the fact that my evening drink(s) were making me unproductive with a dumpy figure.

It all started a couple of years ago in a conversation with one of our sales representatives who was pregnant. She told me she was so glad she had given up smoking a few years earlier, as she was already a non-smoker before she became pregnant. I asked her how she did it and she said she read the Allen Carr book which completely cured her instantly and she'd never thought about it since.

At the time I remember thinking, I'm sure he has also written a book about dieting, maybe I'll look it up at the library. When I was doing this, I saw he had another interesting title called *'No More Hangovers'*. I requested them both, and picked them up next time I was in at the library.

Even though I initially wanted the diet book, I ended up reading *No More Hangovers* first. Because it is a tiny book and very simply written, it didn't take long. A few hours later I remember putting the book down and thinking to myself 'well, I won't be drinking alcohol again'.

I never dreamed that that would be the case, but at this stage it is. I read the book in May 2012 and haven't so much as desired a single sip of alcohol since. I don't really know how this happened and if I ever want to drink again I certainly will, but I just don't want to. It doesn't bother me being around other people drinking and I always, always have a few deep sniffs of a good wine and can really appreciate the bouquet.

I felt like I had to apologise to my husband for ditching him as a 'drinking partner' as we used to enjoy a nice wine together. He says he is fine with it and we have an honest enough relationship that I believe him. He reckons it doesn't bother him in the slightest that I do not drink and even said it has helped him cut back too which he feels better for. On nights when one of us might have poured a drink out of habit, he doesn't. Now he only has wine on the weekends (we would have had drinks 3-5 nights per week before) and the occasional cold beer in summer.

When we visit my native Hawke's Bay which is very much wine country, I still love to visit the vineyards. My husband is a wine enthusiast so I am the happiest person around being the chauffeur showing off our beautiful vineyards while my husband sips. It really was as much fun for me even though I never tasted a drop.

I do miss the taste of my favourite wine varietals don't get me wrong, however I don't want the feeling that comes with drinking now. I have tried de-alcoholised wine but it doesn't bear much resemblance at all.

So what are my new tipples?

If I am in a bar or restaurant after work and want a pick-me-up, for a one-off treat I might order a Red Bull, which I agree isn't very chic sounding, however I always ask for it to be served in a flute. It is a golden colour and looks just like champagne. I've fooled more than one person with my Red Bull in a flute.

In a more casual bar I might order a ginger beer. When we visited Hawaii most bars and restaurants had an alcohol-free beer option – St Pauli and Becks, both German. To me they taste just like normal beer and it's nice not to feel like a kid with a glass of Coke.

I also never feel 'apart' from the drinkers if it's a group of us. Strangely enough I often feel a bit happy along with everyone else later on, as though I've had a few drinks. But I'm just getting into the spirit of things!

We still have cocktail hour at home too. I usually keep in the fridge:

- Diet Coke in a can (I'm not a fan of artificial sweeteners but I don't want to drink sugar. I buy it in cans so I can have a single portion and it's always fizzy).

- Mini bottles of Perrier with Lime or Lemon flavouring (expensive but a yummy and stylish treat).

I serve both the Diet Coke or Perrier in a flute. It feels more special and I sip it slowly, rather than gulp if it was in a big glass. I heard once that apparently French girls called Diet Coke 'Champagne Noir' which probably gave me the idea, impressionable consumer that I am!

- Clausthaler German beer which is 0.5% (classed as alcohol-free) (usually from the bottle on a hot day).

I have any of these and now limit my snacks (cheese and crackers or a little bowl of potato chips) to the weekend. We have our dinner earlier on weeknights and the combination of all these things has helped me to become more svelte. Plus I enjoy my dinner much more not having had snacks beforehand.

If I am going somewhere I might take a few Clausthaler beers, or for a more formal occasion a large bottle of Perrier to have by itself or mix with sparkling grape juice. Always out of a champagne flute of course.

I have had many ask if I am pregnant (no) and look at me strangely (I have learned to live with that). Sometimes I say I am the designated driver, and sometimes that 'I am on a health kick' and it seems to satisfy people. Once you turn down a drink most people want you to have one more than ever.

Really, I can't even tell you have good I feel. My body (and mind) is so happy. I dropped 2-4 kg (5-9 pounds) without even trying. I never wake up seedy anymore. At my age even one glass of wine could affect my sleep and have me feeling below par in the morning. And if you have a 'fun' night where you 'let go', the next day is a guarantee of poor quality eating (at least it was for me) because you feel so rotten.

And it's all down to Allen Carr's book plus, I suppose, my underlying wish to not be beholden to alcohol. I feel so grateful that alcohol no longer has a pull over me. I never hear it calling my name and can walk past any display at the supermarket. I just know 'it's not for me' anymore and that is my wish, not something I am 'trying to stick to'.

My sister who has two young children, read the No More Hangovers book a month after I did and the same thing happened to her. She is an ecstatic non-drinker now. Like me, she used to worry about how much she looked forward to her evening drink, even if she didn't drink that much.

At the time of publishing this ebook, it has been three years since I read Alan Carr's magical book. I don't know how he wrote it to affect me so much, but I can truly say it's a book that has changed my life.

Getting back into sorts

Coming out of winter into spring I'm finding myself quite tired. I am easy to irritate and have been forgetting things. There seems to be a lot going on all around me – at work and home – and I find it overwhelming when I am not my usual self.

I know I've felt like this before and come out of it, but it's not nice to feel out of sorts like I do currently. But just making plans to help myself feels better though. I know that more early nights, less computer time and more good foods (especially protein) will help me get back into balance.

Have you ever heard of adrenal fatigue? I remember going into a health food store and talking with the owner more than a dozen years ago and he told me it sounded like I had that. I had gone in for St John's Wort as I felt quite flat, but he put me onto an adrenal support supplement instead so perhaps I'll invest in another bottle (it isn't too expensive and for me it will just be a short-term thing).

At the moment it feels a bit like my tank is running on empty, and normal everyday interactions and problems can feel like they are getting on top of me.

My life is quite simplified already, both time-wise and possessions-wise, but when I feel like I do now, it doesn't feel like I lead a simple life at all. I long to empty out my rooms at home and have as little as possible around me. Those pictures on minimalist living websites (the pretty rooms, not the stark ones) sound like bliss to me right now.

I know all things to do with nature go in cycles and I know I'm in a strange one right now, but I see it as a good thing. It helps me to know what I want and know how I need to treat myself.

So here is my feel-better plan:

Wonderfully early nights to bed. My husband already knows that I don't feel myself at the moment, so he'll understand. Often he has quite early nights too, so it might be sleepy-time at 9pm (or even earlier) rather than 10pm for a while.

Stay away from junky foods especially sugar (which you crave more when feeling flat I've found) and make sure to include good, natural protein at each meal.

Limit screen-time after dinner. This means I watch one television programme (which is the most I would anyway) and have the laptop shut down before dinner (harder for me than limiting television!).

Investigate the purchase of a bottle of Adrenal Support supplement and start taking those.

Limit caffeine drinks and don't have any caffeine after mid-afternoon.

Walk outside as many days as I can.

Don't leave too long between meals. Sometimes if I'm busy at work it could be 2-3pm before I eat some lunch. Considering I had breakfast at about 8am and a soy latte mid-morning, that's too late. I need to be more organised with having lunch ready to go, rather than get to 1pm and start preparing it (and be ready for the inevitable interruptions that goes with retail).

Tidy up my surroundings (this is mostly to do with work for me at the moment). Because it is coming into the new season we have many deliveries which means unpacking, pricing and photographing for my husband, and 'cutting out' the photos then loading onto the website for me. As well as working in the store, doing all the administration and everything else that comes with running your own business. This means less urgent work is pushed to the background, such as filing, tidying and organising. But those things when left undone contribute to stress, so I am focused on doing the important as well as the urgent work.

Completing small tasks. Don't you find it's the little things, unfinished, that bother you the most? As I go through my day I am endeavouring to complete small tasks as I come across them, and I always receive a boost when I do.

Be around nice people. Keeping away from people that get me down is important because they affect me more when I'm like this. And worry and stress doesn't help you feel better. It's not always possible of course (I have to deal with many different types of people at work), but I've realised that dealing with horrid people who won't be happy no matter what you do can be minimised. It helps me to see it's their problem not mine, and I can limit or eliminate my time with them. Life is just too short to be around nasty people.

Update: I was diagnosed with celiac disease after I wrote this post. I now feel *much* better since I am on a gluten-free diet. It was picked up by a blood test because my iron store was almost empty and I was recommended to have the test by my *sister*, not the doctor. I'd recommend anyone to ask for the gluten/celiac blood test next time they are visiting the doctor for a check-up. Many people go undiagnosed because they don't have obvious symptoms (I didn't).

A WORD FROM THE AUTHOR

Thank you so much for purchasing this book. I do hope you have gained a few good ideas that you can implement into your life.

I welcome feedback and would be grateful if you could leave an honest review at amazon.com.

Please join me for weekly inspiration on living a simple and beautiful French-inspired life at **howtobechic.com** and pick up my free special report **'21 ways to be chic'** while you are there.

ABOUT THE AUTHOR

Fiona Ferris lives in beautiful Auckland, New Zealand with her husband and two rescue-cats. Together, Fiona and her husband run their retail footwear business.

Printed in Great Britain
by Amazon